COMMONSENSE SAILBOAT BUYING

HEWITT SCHLERETH

Henry Regnery Company ● Chicago

Library of Congress Cataloging in Publication Data

Schlereth, Hewitt.
   Commonsense sailboat buying.

   Includes index.
   1. Sailboats.   I. Title.
   VM351.S34   1977   623.82'2   76-42443
   ISBN 8092-8205-4

Copyright © 1977 by Hewitt Schlereth
All rights reserved.
Published by Henry Regnery Company
180 North Michigan Avenue, Chicago, Illinois 60601
Manufactured in the United States of America
Library of Congress Catalog Card Number: 76-42443
International Standard Book Number: 0-8092-8205-4

Published simultaneously in Canada by
Beaverbooks
953 Dillingham Road
Pickering, Ontario LIW 1Z7
Canada

To Deborah, Howard & David

"The days passed happily with me wherever my ship sailed."
—Joshua Slocum

"I could share a lady, but not my boat."
— Anonymous

Contents

Acknowledgments

Many people were very helpful to me in the preparation of this book. While it is not possible to give all their names here, I would like to thank Philip Strenger and A. H. Lovell, who read the manuscript and made many cogent suggestions. Phil also wrote the commentary on the new warranty regulations. Thanks to W. E. Shaw for permission to take the pictures of his production line. Thanks to Peter Schmitt, who acted as consultant for the chapters on marine surveys. Many thanks, too, to Susan Follett and Jody Nichols, who managed to produce a typescript from my handwriting.

Part 1

New Boats

Introduction

The fascination of sailboats is never ending. In 1947 my father taught me to sail, and, in the thirty years since then, I have owned three boats, designed a half-dozen or so, and dreamed of owning countless others.

In 1968 I decided to become a yacht broker, and so instead of being the material of dreams, boats became my livelihood. This fact has made a tremendous difference in the way I look at boats. The fascination is still there, but so is a much more hard-headed and cold-blooded attitude due to the fact that I must constantly and daily assess the value in dollars of every boat I look at.

Sure, my heart still soars when I see the classic shape of a 1930 Alden Schooner. I can admire the superb craftsmanship of her coamings and cap rail. But now I know she'll cost $5,000 a year to maintain, and so I can pass her by. You might say that I'll love her forever — but marriage is out of the question.

Similar considerations go into my view of any new boat — I've got to look at her as a means of earning a living. This means she's got to be reliable. She's also got to be built well and strongly.

These are for the very selfish reason that, if she is not, the person who bought her from me will have her back at my dock being fixed. And that will waste my time and prevent me from using that time to make another sale. Further, the person who bought her from me may think twice about either buying another boat of the same manufacturer or buying another boat from me, the same broker. Because I can't afford either of these to happen, I think you can see that my vantage point on new boats is, necessarily, rather hard-nosed and practical.

New boats today are different from boats of a generation ago not only in the materials used but also in the manner of construction. Thirty years ago boats were handcrafted, built one by one and in strict accordance with very high standards of craftsmanship. In fact, standards were so high and the materials used — primarily the wood — were of such a nature that it was very unusual for the boat to cover up her inner structure.

When you sat inside the boat, her frames, knees, shelves, clamps, carlins and so forth were not only in plain view, they were finished in a way to bring out the natural grain and color of the different woods used. It was an easy matter to assess the strength of her structure.

Today, new boats are primarily fiberglass, which is an excellent material and has made boat ownership possible for many more people because of its relatively low maintenance requirements. Fiberglass, however, can be finished attractively on only one side. Therefore, the essential structure of a modern boat is largely hidden by interior joinery work and fiberglass "liners."

As a result, there is a strong tendency for people to judge the quality of a boat solely on the basis of the appearance of the interior. With few exceptions, this is dangerous.

For the boat's essential qualities are what I as a salesman must evaluate—the strength of her hull, rig, hull-to-deck joint; the reliability of her engine, plumbing, and wiring. These are the things that are going to cause me trouble if they are not right. These are also the things that are going to cause *you* trouble and possibly put you in danger if they are not right.

After all, a boat must be a boat before it is a cozy den. This book will help you learn to look at boats with the critical, unemotional eye of a man who must rely on them for his living.

As I have admitted, I am very aware of the emotional appeal of sailboats. But, before you buy on the basis of this appeal, you need to be in a position to evaluate realistically the really important aspect of a boat—her underlying structure.

Just as you wouldn't buy a house with a knockout kitchen without taking a look at the foundation, wiring, stud-spacing and plumbing, you should not buy a boat without looking at her keel attachments, chain-plate buttresses, hull-deck joint and engine installation.

The aim of this book is to put you in a position to be able to evaluate these fundamental considerations on the basis of what you can observe with your own eyes and feel with your own hands. In other words, with this book I hope to show you how to buy a boat without losing your sanity.

1

Why Buy a Boat, Anyway?

Basically, for two reasons: fun and enjoyment. Sailing is unique in that it is fun in and of itself — you don't have to get anywhere in particular to enjoy it. Just going out and sailing around for a few hours and returning to the same mooring or slip is enjoyable and relaxing.

Beyond this are many levels of adventure to sailing — from the adventure of visiting nearby harbors to the adventure of going far offshore to distant islands or even to other countries.

There is also the aspect of competitive racing, which is a very rapidly expanding part of boating. Finally, there is the grand tradition of yachting, in which a boat is viewed as a quasi-artistic entity and is owned for the beauty of its appearance, finish and joinery as much as for anything else.

Naturally, no one of these elements is purely manifest in any boat. Most boats are a mix of various proportions of speed for racing, comfort for cruising and beautiful interior finish for aesthetic appeal. Today, the racing boats are approaching the point that the preeminent requirement for speed is being met at the sacrifice of other values, principally those that relate to aesthetics and creature comforts.

In many areas of the world, competition has become so keen that the boats are being honed to an even finer degree. The interiors of "hot" racing boats are stripped down to spartan basics. Berths have become canvas stretchers racked one on top of the other, outboard near the transverse centerline, in the interests of optimum weight placement. Heads, or toilets, are left completely out in the open with no concession to even the minimum of privacy that might be provided by a curtain. Galleys are minimal, and there is often no table: meals are basically regarded as a waste of time. The main thing is speed—keeping the boat moving down the course at all times.

These boats are a case of function dominating form, and they are really just a logical result of the demands of racing. On a racing boat a beautiful interior is really a waste: it is expensive, and the money might be better spent on more sails or more powerful winches.

The above remarks are not intended in anyway to deprecate racing boats or to say that racing boats are not suitable for, say, general sailing or family cruising. Quite to the contrary, a boat with a good race record can often be a very satisfactory cruiser.

One thing you can say for a successful racing boat is that for her size she is fast, and a fast boat is very often a boat that is fun to sail. She'll be responsive to the helm and feel alive. She'll very likely be a good sea boat—if she weren't, she wouldn't have her record. She may also be quite strong, because racers are pushed much harder than cruisers and you don't win races if your boat falls apart under stress.

Quite often these days, in fact, a racer and cruiser will have identical hulls and rigs. Their differences will be in the way the interiors are finished and the number and type of winches, sails and other gear that are carried.

So, if you are buying a boat for the fun of sailing, don't be put off by a fin keel and spade rudder. That alone doesn't disqualify the boat as a cruiser. If the design is good and she is strong, she may be an absolute dream under sail and be just the thing for you. Even if you are not planning to race, look at this type of boat. Many have very nice, aesthetically pleasing interiors and comfortable cockpits — and are strong enough to cross an ocean.

The converse of these remarks is also true. There are on the market supposedly strictly cruising designs that are cranky under sail and not built well enough to get out of protected waters. Basically, it is a case of getting your priorities in order and deciding what aspects of a sailboat are most important to you. Here are several things to consider for each of the three categories.

1. Racing: At the very highest levels, this may mean a one-off, custom design with the concomitant high investment, depreciation and expense. At a slightly lower level, it is possible to equip a stock, production racer/cruiser and campaign her with good results. The expense is still high, but depreciation is a great deal less because the boat will find a much broader secondary market when she is no longer competitive.

2. Coastal and protected-water cruising: The well-equipped stock boat discussed above is a good choice, because she will sail well in the typically light-to-moderate winds of summer and does not have to carry the vast amounts of gear and stores required of the ocean voyager. Expense is the lowest of any type, and depreciation will be practically nil if the boat is kept for three to four years.

3. Ocean voyaging: The prime criterion here is *strength,* almost before hull shape or rig. Next in importance is carrying capacity, which the boat must have to be truly independent of

the shore. This boat doesn't necessarily have to be super heavy, but she will probably have to be heavier than an inshore cruiser. As a result, she is likely to be sluggish in light-to-moderate winds.

At this point you might want to skip to Part 2, which is about boat architecture. Read it and study the pictures before you proceed.

Another pleasant aspect of boat ownership that very few people seem to think about is that a boat is one of the few things you can truly own. At some point there comes a time when she is paid for and is yours.

Unlike real estate, there are no annual taxes that must be paid regardless of whether or not the mortgage is paid. For if you pay off the mortgage on a house, the annual taxes mean you are still basically renting the property. Not so with a boat: once she's paid for, she's yours. And, if it ever comes to it, she can be a very cheap house that lets you wander with her, as well.

2

The Financial Side

J. P. Morgan is reputed to have said that if you have to ask how much a boat is going to cost, you can't afford it. Well, this may have been true in the grand days when a yacht was at least 100 feet long and as much a work of art as anything else. As works of art they cost stupendous amounts of money to create and equally grand amounts to maintain.

But today's sailboats are made from much less exotic and costly materials. The general maintenance required is basically scrubbing, painting and varnishing. Today's boats are much much smaller and, relative to the income of their owners, probably take up no more of a percentage of that income than J. P.'s yachts did of his. If you can spare 10 to 15 percent of your income per year, you can very probably own a decent-sized sailboat.

About four thousand people in this country buy new cruising sailboats in the 26- to 40-foot range each year; probably three times that number buy used boats in this same size range. If you have an income of $25,000 a year, you can in all probability be one of them. And many people who own boats manage on a great deal less income than that.

Having said all this, it is still a fact that cruising sailboats are expensive as sin. To be more accurate, they require a large captial investment. You may well wonder why it is you can buy a 22-foot car with 3000 moving parts for $6,000 when a 22-foot sailboat with maybe 100 moving parts costs around $9,000.

The fundamental reason is that cars are produced in vast quantities. Boats, on the other hand, are produced in dribs and drabs. A large sailboat manufacturer, for example, produces only six hundred boats per year and has a total sales volume of only about $12 million. This is small potatoes compared to General Motors or Ford with their sales in the millions of units and billions of dollars. Since boat production costs have to be spread over very few units, the price of each unit is necessarily high.

The positive side to this is that, because sailboats are basically very simple and built of very durable materials, there is very little to wear out. Consequently, they last a long time. Sails on a cruising boat, for instance, can be expected to be serviceable for ten years, given reasonable care. This means that depreciation is very low and, in fact, is offset to a large extent by inflation.

To take an example, suppose you buy a new 30-footer this year for a total investment of $22,000. You keep it for three years and then decide to sell it or trade it in for a larger boat. What is your boat worth?

Well, it is worth what the market is willing to pay for it, and the market process works something like this: three years have passed and the price of a new boat like yours is now $26,000. Your boat is in top shape, shiny and very sparkling. A used-boat buyer has the choice of buying your boat or a new one. What does the dollar saving have to be in order for him to buy your boat?

In part, it will depend on how much a given amount of money is worth to him. But he'll almost certainly buy your boat for $20,000, thereby saving $6,000. He'll probably pay $21,000 if it is exceptionally appealing. For more than that, he'll probably opt for the new boat.

You can see that, unless you consider things like present value and discounted cash flow, you can come out pretty reasonably on the capital investment side of owning a boat.

Now, what about the expense side of boat owning? That is, the money that has to be laid out to cover the operating costs, which are the irrecoverable dollars involved in boat owning. These are the cash expenditures for things like slip or mooring space, winter storage, bottom paint and insurance.

These things are going to vary somewhat from area to area, but, since things like slip space, bottom painting, rigging and such are levied on a per-foot basis in most boating areas, it is easy enough to run them down and add them up. In our area, western Long Island Sound, the operating costs of a fiberglass auxiliary sailboat run about $60 per foot per year. This includes insurance, summer and winter space and presumes that the boat owner does only the basic cleaning of the boat and waxing the hull.

In other areas of the country this figure is going to vary — indeed, it is a good deal lower in eastern Long Island Sound, only 60 miles away.

If you are able to do things like painting the bottom of your boat yourself, maintaining the engine, washing and storing the sails and so forth, you can reduce the annual upkeep cost of an inboard-powered 30-footer to quite small proportions. Here is how the annual expenses break down in western Long Island Sound, one of the most expensive areas in the country in which to own a boat.

Insurance	$350
Summer slip space at $20/foot	600
Hauling, unrigging, preparing for winter	160

Winter storage space	360
Storage for spars	40
Build frame for cover	45
Uncover in spring	25
Paint bottom	125
Launch and rig	90
Commission engine and water system	50
	$1,845

Now, obviously, many items here could be done by you, the owner. For example, you could build the frame for the winter cover or, for that matter, leave the boat uncovered—fiberglass is very durable, remember. You could also paint the bottom, prepare the engine and water system for winter and put the engine and water system back into commission in the spring.

Such savings can be approximated:

Preparing for winter	$ 60
Frame for cover	45
Uncover in spring	25
Paint bottom	100
Commission engine and water system	50
	$280

You might also find a boat yard in which you could store the boat without taking out the mast and, instead of at a slip, keep the boat on a mooring or join a yacht club in which these things are included. Many yacht clubs, even in our area, have annual dues of less than $600.

All in all, you could cut your total maintenance bill down from the hypothetical $60 to about $35 per foot by doing as much of the work as you can yourself. Over the years, I've found that most people really enjoy puttering on their boats and doing things themselves. It's part of the pleasure of the whole activity.

To return to the investment part of boat ownership, you saw

what you were likely to recover if you held a boat three years. Suppose you bought a boat and, for one reason or another, wanted to sell it after one year. What would the numbers look like then? About 15 percent less than you paid for it — roughly $3,000. Again, this is the spread that a buyer would need in order to choose the used boat rather than a new one.

This 15 percent figure is an interesting one because it is the minimum down payment required by companies that specialize in boat financing. Apparently they, too, figure that about 85 percent of the cost of a sailboat would be recoverable even if the boat had to be sold within a year of purchase.

Many people are surprised to find that you can finance so much of a new sailboat. Not only that, loan terms are quite commonly seven to ten years. It is actually easier to buy a boat than a house. I know that many people feel it is practically immoral to finance something like a boat, but the fact is that most boats are financed (although not normally to the full 85 percent), often by the very people who could put the whole chunk of capital into the boat if they wanted.

I suspect these individuals have their money working in places where it grows more rapidly than the interest they pay to borrow on the boat. Too, I am sure that the financing institutions have a very low loss rate on sailboat financing. For instance, in the past seven years only one boat sold by our company was repossessed. And the financing firm not only was able to sell the boat, it recovered every nickel it was owed.

Boat financing works very much like car financing: the interest you pay is called "add-on" interest and the true interest is higher than the nominal or stated rate. An example is the easiest way to explain this: suppose you have decided to buy a 30-foot production fiberglass sailboat and the investment required, including tax, is $23,000. You are going to pay $5,000 down and finance the remaining $18,000 for ten years. The nominal interest rate is 7.5 percent add-on. Here is the way the numbers work out:

Amount borrowed	$18,000
Interest rate	× .075
Interest per year	1,350
Term of loan	× 10 years
Total interest	$13,500

The total interest of $13,500 is now added-on to the $18,000 you are borrowing, and this is what you are actually paying:

Principal	$18,000
Interest	13,500
Total amount to be repaid	$31,500

Since you are going to be repaying in monthly installments, there will be 120 monthly payments in 10 years of $262.50 each.

The thing to notice about this type of interest is that the amount of interest does not decline as you repay the loan. It is always $13,500. Since, in effect, you only have use of half the money because you repay as you go and not all at once at the end of the 10 years, the equivalent simple interest rate is nearly double the nominal rate. Thus, borrowing at 7½ percent add-on is approximately equivalent to borrowing at a simple interest rate of 13 percent.

Naturally, there are less expensive ways of financing a boat. Among them are the following:

1. Taking advantage of the increased value of your house to remortgage it, thus borrowing the money at simple interest with a very long-term repayment schedule.

2. Pledging stocks or bonds as security for the money. Again, this is borrowing at simple interest.

3. Pledging a savings account as security and borrowing at simple interest rates against that.

These alternatives are appealing because the interest is usually about one-half of the effective rate with add-on. However, in the event you default, the lender under the above three options has either your house, your bonds or your savings account. You end up with the boat.

Under the add-on method, the lender ends up with the boat and must go to the bother and expense of selling it to recover his money. Thus, because his risk is higher, so is the interest he charges.

At the risk of striking a negative note, this seems like an appropriate place to advise that, before you get involved in the whole process of looking for and buying a sailboat, you very squarely ask yourself which you like more, money or sailing. You might be surprised at the number of people who immerse themselves in boat hunting and obviously never face this question until the crunch comes: they've found the ideal boat for them, they can afford it, but it means taking X out of the savings account. At this final moment, they discover they love the money in the bank more than they can imagine loving the boat in the water. Talk about frustration and a waste of time!

Presuming you have crossed this hurdle, let's move on to another money item which comes up in buying a boat—sales taxes and what is involved if you decide you want to avoid them.

Briefly, if you own an auxiliary sailboat, you are required by law to register it either with the state in which you will principally use the boat or with the U.S. Coast Guard in whose district the boat will be principally used. If you register it in a state that has a sales tax, you will have to pay tax to that state. Thus, the only way to avoid sales tax is to register your boat with a state—or a state in a Coast Guard district—where there is no sales tax.

One state that does not have a sales tax is Delaware, but if you think you can, for example, buy a boat in New York from an individual and register it in Delaware, you should know that Delaware will require a statement from you to the effect that Delaware will be the place where you will principally use the boat.

So, unless you are willing to lie a little, there are great difficulties in trying to avoid sales tax. And, with all states scrambling for revenue these days, you can bet it is going to get more and more difficult. In addition, some states such as Connecticut have personal property taxes, which are levied annually.

Taking the long view of this problem, it seems foolish to me to go through contortions to avoid tax. After all, one of the reasons you're buying a boat is to avoid some of the hassles of modern life. Why leave yourself open to a potential future hassle with the government?

Pay them their pound of flesh and enjoy your boat with an easy mind. A boat is one of the few things in this world that you can own outright, so make the most of it and don't give the tax group a chance to get their hands on it.

3

Putting Your Priorities in Order

In my preface I made the statement that "a boat must be a boat before it is a cozy den." Now I want to expand on this a bit.

A boat lives in an element — water — alien to man, and when you set out in one you trust your life to it in a way that you don't in a car or other land vehicle. What are inconveniences in land travel are very often the stuff of tragedies at sea.

For instance, the loss of motive power in a car means a more or less extended stay on the side of the road. Inconvenient, but not particularly dangerous. The loss of the rig in a sailboat is extremely grave.

Similarly, a sudden squall with high winds and rain may mean that the motorist has to pull to the side of the road until it passes by. But a sailboat has to make progress in these conditions and must cope with them directly and without shelter. It seems obvious, therefore, that some things must be sought first in a boat and others relegated to lesser priority.

By this I do not mean to say that a sailboat has to be a spartan, sterile machine — not in the least. A boat can be a good strong boat *and* a cozy den. But, given a choice between a strong structure and beautiful woodwork, common sense says you have to choose the structure first, since that's what you're really going to sea in.

To reduce this concept to an absurdity, imagine a steel boat with a couple of pipe berths lined up next to a boat with a hand-rubbed mahogany interior and a papier-mâché hull. In which are you going to set out to sea?

That example is occasioned by the tendency I have observed over the years for people to judge a boat by its interior. This is very much like judging a book by its cover or a house by its kitchen. After all, the people who are building houses and boats are no fools. If kitchens sell houses and interiors sell boats, that's where a lot of money is going to go. And maybe, just maybe, it's going to go there at the expense of other things.

It is possible to have a strong boat and an interior that is a work of art. But remember that art is expensive and if you basically only want to go sailing, perhaps you can do without that part of yachting.

In any case, the set of priorities I suggest is this:

Crucial Importance:

> Good design
> Strong hull
> Strong rig

High Importance:

> Layout
> Good engine
> Good plumbing
> Good electrical system

The problem before you is to come up with some ways that

you, using your own eyes and hands, can form an accurate judgment of these factors. We'll deal with first things first.

Design

This is probably the most difficult thing for a newcomer to sailing to assess, since the overall design of the boat is the result of a blend of compromises between speed, room, looks, handling, cost and many other factors. After you've messed around with boats for a few years, you will develop a critical eye. But, assuming at this point you are a relative newcomer, here are a few ideas.

1. *Find out how long the boat you are looking at has been in production and how many have been made.* The serial number of the boat is usually stamped on a metal plate mounted in the cockpit. If you find out that the boat you are looking at has been in production for, say, 5 years and you're standing in number 1,000, that's a lot of boats and a healthy market life.

For sailboats of 26 to 35 feet, an average yearly production of 50 or more units and four years of continuous production indicates very good market acceptance. If the boat were a bad design or had cranky sailing characteristics, it might reach a high level for one year (due to an exceptionally low price, perhaps), but it just wouldn't hang in there year after year.

Since November 1972, all boats have been required to have their serial number and model year molded into an upper corner of the transom.

2. *Certain designers consistently produce good boats.* By this I mean boats that sail well and do not have bad characteristics such as a vicious weather or lee helm. Sometimes it happens that the execution of these designs by the builders leaves something to be desired — but more of this in later chapters. These I consider to be among the good designers of production fiberglass boats.

Ted Brewer
Cuthbertson and Cassian
Halsey Herreshoff
Ted Hood
Bruce King
William Lapworth
Charley Morgan
Gary Mull
William Shaw
Sparkman and Stephens
William Tripp

3. *Stand in the cockpit of the boat and try to determine if the designer made adequate provision for moving around on deck.* Are the decks wide enough to go forward on? Is the cockpit large enough for the number of people who can reasonably be expected to go cruising on the boat? Remember, you spend a lot of time in the cockpit of a sailboat. To this end, are the coamings high enough to provide reasonable back support and comfort?

4. *Go below and see if the layout is a workable one.* One test I always apply is to ask myself if there is a comfortable place to sit or sleep in heavy weather. This means there should be at least one berth near midship, where the motion is least in a seaway. It may require a leeboard on one tack, but it shouldn't require converting from a dinette. This is one reason I like boats with tables that fold away against a bulkhead—this layout usually gives two berths port and starboard in the middle of the boat. No matter which way the boat is heeled, you can rest.

The above considerations pretty well rule out any but aft galley in the general size range we're talking about (26 to 40 feet). In larger craft it becomes possible to locate the galley elsewhere because it becomes possible to provide comfortable seating and/or sleeping space also, due to the greater space available. But for smaller boats the aft galley is practically a must. It can be on one side or spread on both sides.

The reasons for this are basically that the cook has access to the cockpit for passing food and for communicating, the heat from the stove logically vents through the companionway, there is a large flow of fresh air for the cook, the cook does not block the passageway through the boat and can readily brace himself in place using either a webbed belt or the companionway ladder, or both.

Admittedly, these remarks leave very little flexibility for the layout. I think this is proper and due to the fact that much of the layout is dictated by the practical realities facing a craft that must be lived on, dined on and slept on while in motion — often violent motion.

Having said this much about design and layout, I am going to digress into a description of how a fiberglass sailboat is made and then cover the remaining points on the hull, rig, engine, plumbing and electrical system in Chapter Five.

4

How a Fiberglass Boat Is Made

As I mentioned earlier, the fiberglass sailboat industry is a relatively small one. Actual production in terms of units rarely exceeds six hundred per year for even the largest manufacturer of cruising sailboats in the 22- to 40-foot range.

This low production is due to two factors. First, the market is small—only about four thousand new sailboats in this size range are bought each year in the entire country. Second, each boat is largely built by hand, much the way cars were before Henry Ford. This is largely because of the nature of the construction.

Contrary to what many people think, a fiberglass boat is not a homogeneous piece of plastic, such as a Clorox bottle or one of those plastic model kits your kids put together. A fiberglass boat is a combination layer cake and jigsaw puzzle: each layer has to be put in by hand and the entire boat must be assembled in large part by hand.

You might think from my remarks that the largest part of

the cost of a fiberglass sailboat would be the labor involved, but this is not the case. It only takes, for instance, about three hundred man hours to build a 30-foot auxiliary sailboat from start to finish — about ten days in a well-run plant.

The cost of these man hours is only about 25 percent of the cost of the boat. The other 75 percent is primarily materials, so you can see that a major way to reduce the cost of a boat is to reduce the amount of material in the boat — or to substitute cheaper materials, or to opt for a less plush interior in order to maintain a strong hull.

Once the boat is put together, however, it is very difficult to determine how thick the hull is, i.e., how much material went into it. There are ways, though, to make reasonable deductions about this and we will get to them in the next chapter. For now, let's see just how a fiberglass sailboat is made.

The process really begins with the decision to come out with a new model. The general size of the boat and desirable features are indicated to the designer or design group, who produce preliminary drawings for the top management or whoever is responsible for the overall direction of the new boat.

Often, at this point, these plans are discussed with certain dealers for their ideas, criticisms and suggestions. Over a period of months, the design is finalized and the job of getting it into production begins.

The first thing that is actually built is what is called the hull plug. This is usually made upside down of wood in very much the same manner that a wood boat is constructed. When complete, it is an exact model of the hull of the new boat. This is sanded and polished to a high finish and then waxed. A hard, enamel-like coating called gel-coat is sprayed onto the waxed plug, and then sheets of fiberglass are laid onto the gel-coat and saturated with resin which hardens and forms a skin over the plug about 1/8-inch thick.

More layers of fiberglass are put on, saturated with resin

and allowed to harden. One of the characteristics of the fiberglass sandwich that is being built up over the plug is that it is quite flexible, and so many layers are needed to ensure rigidity. When the desired thickness is reached—about ½-inch or so—a framework is built around the structure to further ensure stiffness, and it is separated from the plug.

This is the mold for the hulls of the new boat. Often, if the new model is expected to sell in large numbers, another mold will be made. In a similar manner, other molds are made for the deck and such other components as the cabin sole (floor), galley and berth platforms.

Space is now allocated in the plant and the molds are moved to the far end, or beginning, of the production line. Before actual construction of a boat begins, the mold is thoroughly cleaned and heavily waxed to ensure that the hull, when completed, will come out of the mold and not stick in it.

The first layer to go into the mold is the outermost layer of the finished hull, the gel-coat. This is the layer that has the color of the finished boat, although its main purpose is to provide a hard, dense layer that will resist abrasion and prevent water penetration. This is sprayed onto the inside surface of the mold by a man operating a special spray gun that does not use air. This ensures that the gel-coat goes on as densely as possible.

Now, since this gel-coat is very hard when dry, it is also quite brittle. Fiberglass is flexible so it is necessary that the gel-coat be quite thin. Too thick and it may craze, or develop hairline cracks as the completed boat flexes in use. This is an area where good supervision and operator skill are required.

After the gel-coat has had time to set, the first layer of fiberglass is laid into the mold. This is usually the type of glass known as "mat," which consists of loosely woven strands about 4 inches long. In appearance it is a little like straw. The mat is saturated with resin, and any air bubbles are rolled out.

Mat can also be applied in another way, and that is by a

machine that takes a thread of fiberglass, cuts it into short lengths, applies resin and blows the strands onto the mold. This is the infamous chopper gun.

Its advantage is that it saves time; but the thickness of the mat laid down is controlled by the operator and so may be applied too thickly or thinly. Many builders use a combination of cut mat and gun. For structural parts of the boat such as hull and deck, they will have the mat cut out of large rolls and placed by the mold where they can be counted as they are put into the boat to ensure that a hull of the designed thickness is built.

The next layer into the mold is a layer of woven roving that is made of thick fiberglass threads woven together much like a cane chair. Because the threads have a slick texture, the material has much the same look and feel as medieval chain mail. This material is the strength of the boat; the principal reason for the mat is to bind the layers of roving together. Because of its slick texture, two layers of roving will not bind well directly to one another.

Construction is continued by laying in alternating layers of mat and roving until the specified hull thickness is reached. This will vary from the deck edge to the keel. On a 30-footer, the thickness at the deck will probably be about ¼ inch while at the keel it may be as much as ¾ inch. This, of course, varies from manufacturer to manufacturer and is very difficult to ascertain. Again, there are ways to form some conclusions; we'll get to them in the next chapter.

Just as a personal observation, I always like to see roving the last layer inside the hull because, to me, that means the hull has been finished with a strength layer rather than a fill or binder layer like mat.

As I have indicated, the roving-mat-resin sandwich is basically flexible. So, to achieve a desirable level of stiffness, many layers have to be built up, depending upon the engineering requirements. For example, the hull is going to need to be most rigid where the concentrated weight of the ballast is to be carried. It can be thinner at the deck edge because considerable stiffness will be imparted by the attachment of the hull to the deck.

There are other ways to achieve rigidity in a hull. One of these is to use a different type of roving. Woven roving is relatively cheap and, even though many layers have to be built up to achieve stiffness and strength, it is still cheaper than what is called unidirectional roving.

In unidirectional roving, instead of having the thread bundles run at right angles to each other, they all run longitudinally and are only lightly stitched together crossways. The effect is like piling up straws, one on top of another. You get a very light structure that is very rigid and strong in the fore-and-aft dimension.

Using this material, it is possible to build a much lighter hull without sacrificing structural strength. Even though this hull will be more expensive than one employing the more traditional roving, lightness has its advantages (see Part 2) and several builders employ this method of achieving it.

To return to our hull. At this point, it is complete and still inside the mold. Before it has completely cured, while it is still "green," certain structural members are installed. These usually consist of plywood pieces that are glassed onto the inside of the hull to reinforce the stem and transom areas, for example, and to provide the bases onto which the chain plates will be bolted. It is important that these items be done before the hull is completely cured, for in that way the strongest bond is assured.

This process is called the "secondary bonding" and is an important area to look at when you are evaluating the quality of the workmanship that went into the boat. These secondary bonds should be smooth, without bubbles or "icicles" (sharp strands of cured glass and resin) and should flow almost imperceptibly onto the final layer of the hull itself. Done this way, maximum spreading of the loads on these members is assured and so maximum strength.

At this point, the engine beds and the stern tube for the propeller shaft are often glassed in, too. If the ballast is going to be contained within the cavity of the keel, it is placed and sealed in with roving, mat and resin. Once this work is done, the hull is removed from the mold, placed on a cradle and wheeled from the molding area to the line along which the final work will be done.

Unkike a car production line, a boat is not continuously moving. Rather, the boat sits in the same spot—often for days—while certain things are done. Then it is moved ahead to another stage where it may also remain for a day or more. Indeed, some builders only move the hull once—out of the mold—and not again until the boat is complete and ready to go out of the door.

Now, while the hull was being molded in one area, the deck and hull and deck liners were being molded in another.

Unlike the hull, which is usually composed of many layers of glass, the deck is a sandwich of glass and either plywood or balsa. This is because the deck needs to be light and more rigid than the hull, and this is the most practical way to achieve these two qualities. Lightness is sought so that the weight of the deck, being up high, will not work any more than necessary against the stability of the boat; rigidity is wanted because it adds greatly to the strength of the hull-deck combination. Besides, who would want to walk around on a spongy deck?

Usually, the deck is turned over and, while the engine and structural bulkheads (walls) are being installed in the hull, the head liner is bonded to the deck. This liner is not a structural part of the boat. Its purpose is to cover up the underside of the deck so that a pleasing, finished ceiling is overhead in the completed interior. Often the head liner is made entirely of chopped mat by the chopper gun.

Once the head liner is on, various items of deck hardware such as stanchions, cleats and winches are attached. The cockpit is also a part of the deck mold, and, if the boat is to have a steering wheel, this is mounted while the deck is upside down. Now the deck can be attached to the hull. And it is at this stage that boat manufacturers begin to diverge from one another.

If the boat is to have great attention paid to the interior, the deck and hull will be mated and then a crew of cabinetmakers will take over the boat and build, item by item, the berths, lockers, drawers and so forth and install and finish them. Obviously, this process is costly; a boat done in this manner can have up to half of its total cost represented by the interior.

For this reason, most production builders do as much of the interior as they can elsewhere in the plant and install the interior before joining the hull and deck. In this way, much time and labor are saved, there is little post-finishing and, once the hull and deck are joined, the boat is virtually complete, needing only the mast and boom from the rigging shop and, possibly, the berth cushions from the upholstery shop.

Now, at this point we have built boat Number 1 of a hypothetical series of boats. It is here that industry practices again diverge and vary. When this Number 1 hull came out of the mold, some builders would have immediately begun Number 2 so that, by the time Number 1 was ready to go out the door, Numbers 2, 3, 4 and 5 would probably be lined up in various stages of completion — or disarray.

A more conservative practice, however, is followed by other builders and that is this: before they start Number 2, they completely assemble Number 1, rig it, launch it and sail it to see if, for example, the rig is in the right place so that the boat does not have a vicious weather or lee helm. Normally, with an established, experienced builder, the design is fine and so series production begins.

But sometimes little kinks do turn up and needed changes

can be made before the boat is sold to the retail buyer (you). It's so nice to know, when you set off on your first sail in your new boat if the design is in its first year of production, that someone — one hopes the designer — has been out in the beast before you and that you are not playing test pilot to somebody's dream of what a boat should be. That is to say that you have bought a verified, true boat and not merely what someone hopes is a boat.

Further Reading

Should you feel that you want to go deeper into the details of fiberglass boat construction, this book is, in my opinion, a good one to read: *Boatbuilding and Repairing with Fiberglass* by Melvin D. C. Willis. Camden, Maine: International Marine Publishing Co., 177 pages.

1. Mold room from above. Molds covered with polyethelene have been waxed preparatory to beginning construction. Mold in middle with cross-members is completed hull curing.

2. View of center hull from aft. Ballast is in place and secondary bonding has begun—cabin floor support between first and second crosspieces.

3. Near hull has just been laid up. Note how shiny and black are insides of upper mold. (Black is used because it reveals minor imperfections.)

4. Mat and woven roving. Roving is on right.

5. Mat and woven roving. Mat is hanging down on left.

6. & 7. Completed hulls just out of the mold.

8. Interior that has been built in another part of the plant.

9. Interior in hull.

10. Interior bulkheads (walls) being bonded to hull.

11. View down a line. Near boat is having interior installed. Rear boat is having basic secondary bonding done and engine installed.

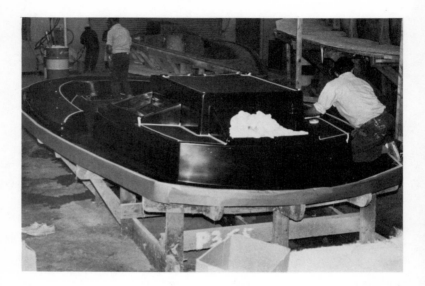

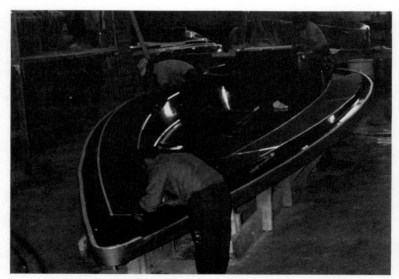

12. & 13. Deck mold being prepared to begin building on decks.

14. Deck laid up. Hump to rear is cockpit.

15. Head liner mold with head liner laid up.

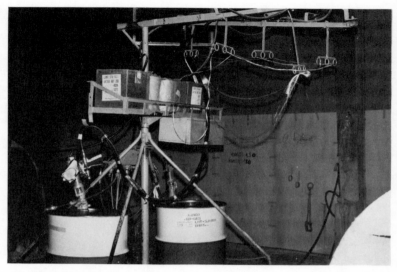

16. The infamous chopper gun. Glass thread comes from upper boxes and resin and catalyst from the drums.

17. Head liner mated to deck. This is done while deck is still in mold to prevent distortion.

18. Deck removed from mold and turned over. Installation of deck hardware is underway.

19. Hull deck joint before finishing with metal "C" rail and vinyl cover, and glassing inside seam.

20. Another view down the line.

5

Clues

As you can gather from the preceding chapter and pictures, once the boat is all together, it is very difficult to determine some things — such as how thick the hull is. Since you are going to be shopping among completed boats in a dealer's showroom, you are going to have to assess the construction from what you can see. These things I call clues; they are basically the things you can see as you move around the boat. We'll start from the outside.

Exterior of Hull

The exterior surface of the hull should be as dense, smooth, hard and shiny as the surface of a new billiard ball. If it looks like the skin of an orange or has a dull, porous look, it is a sign of either inferior material (gel-coat) or incorrect application — possibly due to inexperience on the part of the spray-gun operator, poor supervision, or the fact that the hull mold needed cleaning and refinishing.

43

In addition to having a good surface texture, the entire surface of the hull should sweep in fair curves from bow to stern with few if any hard spots. A good way to judge the fairness of the hull is to look from underneath along the rail-line where hull and deck join — to see that it is an even curve from bow to stern without large flat sections. Occasionally, a bulkhead will cause a crease to appear in the exterior of the hull; this is probably not serious if there are not too many of them. This is a test of the general care with which the boat was built. If you are considering a dark-colored hull, try to find another from the same builder to look at, as black or dark hulls magnify every flaw of this kind.

I personally like to see a slight print-through of the woven roving in the hull, because that tells me it is there and probably in sufficient quantity. This material, you remember, is the strength component of the fiberglass sandwich. If, however, the hull looks, to a casual glance, like a waffle, excessive heat was allowed to build up in the mold during construction and the appearance and hence the value of the boat suffer. Print-through of the roving pattern should be visible only to a very careful scrutiny from close range.

While you are outside the boat, it might be a good idea to find out what the ballast material is — ask if the brochure doesn't say — and how it is attached to the hull. Lead is the densest readily available material and so it is the preferred ballast material. Being dense, a relatively great weight can be concentrated in a small volume placed low where it will contribute best to the stability of the boat.

I like to see the ballast either attached to or set inside a keel which is formed as part of the hull, in the manner that a branch grows from a tree. This spreads the load over a larger area of the bottom of the hull than would be the case if the ballast were simply attached directly to the bottom of the boat. If the keel is cast and bolted to the hull, the seam should be narrow and the bolts (visible in the bilge) massive and spread over a noticeably wide reinforced area.

Lead is expensive and so, in many of the smaller production boats, cast iron is used. There is a little more maintenance with this material for, after a season in the water, the iron is going to show rust spots that will need to be wire-brushed out and primed before a new coat of bottom paint is applied.

Normally, today, the cast iron is in the form of the entire keel of the boat and is bolted directly to the bottom of the hull. If you are looking at a boat with such a keel, make a note to check inside for substantial reinforcement to take the more concentrated load of such an installation.

While you are under the boat, you should try to determine the size of the rudder stock, the metal shaft to which the rudder is attached to the boat. On a free-standing spade rudder, it needs to be substantial, because it takes the entire steering load.

Here it is purely a case of comparing one boat to another. If you find one boat that has a substantially smaller rudder stock than another, it may indicate — along with other facts — that the builder is skimping. Similarly, look to see how the builder engineered the stock's entry into the hull. It should be well-secured. A poorly secured stock can result in the rudder's falling out of the boat. Poor engineering also can lead to a leak which is difficult to reach and fix.

In the Cockpit

One of the first things I look at when I get into the cockpit is the seat lockers. Not how capacious they are, but how the hatches are made. I like to see deep scuppers around the hatch allowing drainage to keep out as much water as possible, and I like to see deep sides on the hatch for the same reason. I look at the size of the hinges (Photos 21 and 22) and whether they are bolted on or simply screwed or riveted in place.

Inside the seat lockers is one place you can usually see the inside of the hull and, as I said, I like it if the last layer is roving instead of mat. The inside of the lockers also reveals whether the general level of fiberglass work is neat or sloppy.

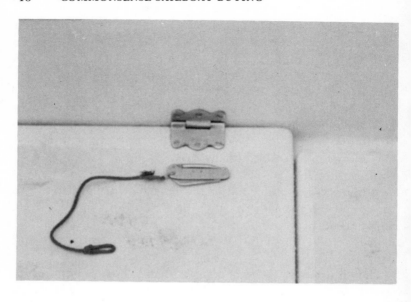

21. & 22. Another clue: the size of the hinges on the seat lockers.

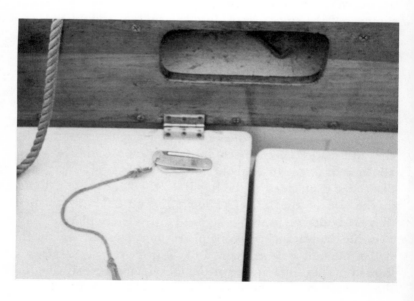

While in the cockpit, check the size — i.e., diameter of the
lifelines. You will be amazed how much this varies from
manufacturer to manufacturer. I like hefty lifelines — at least
¼ inch in diameter. Take hold of a stanchion and pull firmly.
Fiberglass is flexible, but the deck should not move more than
fractionally — here again, it's a matter of comparing one boat
to another more than a matter of absolutes. If you hear some
crackling noises while you do this, it's normal for
fiberglass — it's the brittle gel-coat making noises for the same
reason cellophane does when you crumple it.

Look at the sizes of the cleats and winches. Are they substantial compared to others you've noted? Are they through-
bolted?

On Deck

Look at the size of the chain plates, the metal bars to which
the shrouds are attached when the mast is installed. How do
they compare with others you've seen on the same size boat?
How strongly are they secured below deck? They must
withstand enormous strain.

I remember once I was trying to sell a certain 30-footer to a
man who had obviously never noticed chain plate sizes before.
The 30-footer was tied up next to a 40-footer and I asked him
to compare their chain plates. He was amazed to find that
those on the 30-footer were just as large!

Now, the 30-footer was certainly overbuilt in this area, but
this is an area that I like to see overbuilt. Those bars of
stainless, well-tied into the hull, are what keep the entire rig
in the boat. Overbuilding in this area may indicate a respect
for Mother Sea that will also show up in overbuilding in other
areas.

Look at the hatches. Do they seem as if they will do a good
job of keeping water out? How do they compare with others?

How does the toe rail look? If it is teak, is it substantial or
skimpy? The hull and deck of many boats are fastened

together through the toe rail, so if it is wood there should be some heft or "meat" to it. The same considerations hold if the toe rail is a metal extrusion.

Inside

As you go below, into the boat, take a look at the companionway hatch. Does it slide easily? Does it seem well-made? Strong enough for a person to stand on safely? Is there a spray-shielding cover in front of it to keep water from coming in under the lip?

Once you are below, take a close look at the joinery work. Is it nicely fitted together and made, or is the craftsmanship of the cabinets, called "quality," just a layer of varnish with raised grain that feels bumpy and sandy to the touch? How about the overhead? Is it smooth and fair? If it is not a durable material such as fiberglass, will it be easy to remove or replace if it gets stained by a leak or ripped by accident?

Look in the hanging locker. This is one place in the boat where you can usually see enough to assess the secondary bonding. Usually, this is where the buttresses are to which the chain plates are bolted. Is it smooth or fair without "icicles" and trapped bubbles? Is it neat work? Does the bulkhead (wall) seem to be well-bonded to the hull with roving? The tests here are the same as for any secondary bonding.

The hull-deck joint is usually visible from inside the hanging locker, and on pages 49 to 54 I have arranged (in order of probable strength) sketches of various typical methods of attaching the hull and decks. As I indicated in the previous chapter, this is the largest seam in a fiberglass boat, and it is important that it be not only watertight but strong, since the deck contributes mightily to the finished strength of the whole boat. Consider the size and spacing of the bolts or screws used in any of these methods and compare boat to boat.

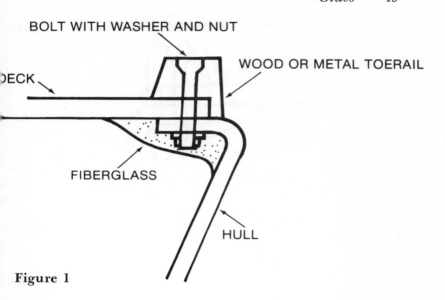

BOLT WITH WASHER AND NUT

DECK

WOOD OR METAL TOERAIL

FIBERGLASS

HULL

Figure 1

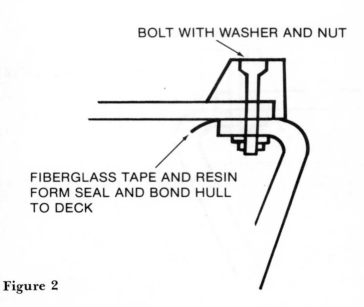

BOLT WITH WASHER AND NUT

FIBERGLASS TAPE AND RESIN
FORM SEAL AND BOND HULL
TO DECK

Figure 2

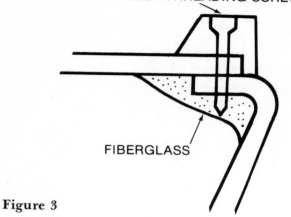

SELF-THREADING SCREW

FIBERGLASS

Figure 3

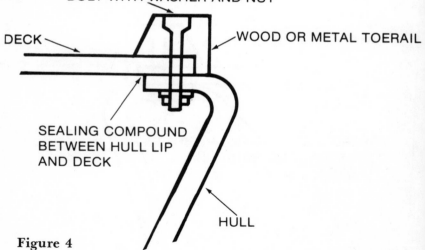

BOLT WITH WASHER AND NUT

DECK

WOOD OR METAL TOERAIL

SEALING COMPOUND
BETWEEN HULL LIP
AND DECK

HULL

Figure 4

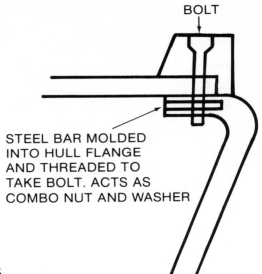

BOLT

STEEL BAR MOLDED
INTO HULL FLANGE
AND THREADED TO
TAKE BOLT. ACTS AS
COMBO NUT AND WASHER

Figure 5

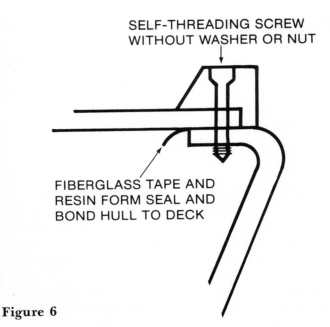

SELF-THREADING SCREW
WITHOUT WASHER OR NUT

FIBERGLASS TAPE AND
RESIN FORM SEAL AND
BOND HULL TO DECK

Figure 6

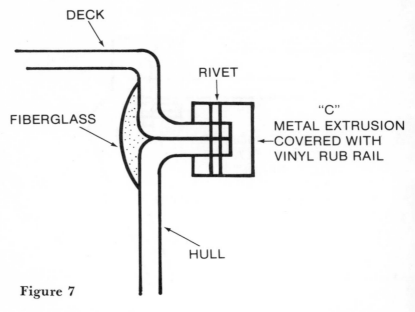

Figure 7

As a way to get an overview of the structural parts of the boat and to clarify the whole thing in your mind, you might imagine that the boat is a shoe box. You know that without the lid (deck) on the shoe box, its sides are very floppy. You can see that if you put the lid on the box and fasten it to the sides of the box, the sides will become stiffer and stronger.

In addition to the lid, a heavy keel is also going to have to be fastened to the bottom of the box. You can see, therefore, that the bottom of the box is going to have to be thicker than the sides and, additionally, may need internal bracing to help stiffen the bottom and spread the load. Similar considerations apply to the attachment parts (chain plates) for the shrouds (the wires that help support the mast). Their attachments, called buttresses or gussets, should be large enough to spread the loads and carefully bonded to the inside of the hull to ensure maximum strength.

The next thing you may want to check are the through-hull fittings, the fittings at those points where the drains from the

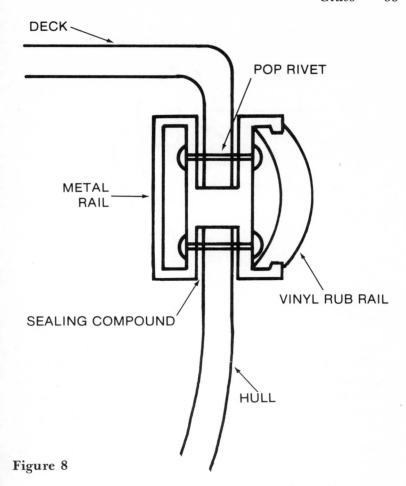

DECK

POP RIVET

METAL RAIL

VINYL RUB RAIL

SEALING COMPOUND

HULL

Figure 8

sinks and the toilets go out through the hull and where the engine-cooling water and toilet-flushing water come in. There should be a shut-off valve at each of these points, and the most important point to note is whether or not the fitting is mounted on a backing block to properly distribute the loads imparted in mounting and using it.

Great argument has raged as to whether these valves should be sea cocks or gate valves. Gate valves work like the outside

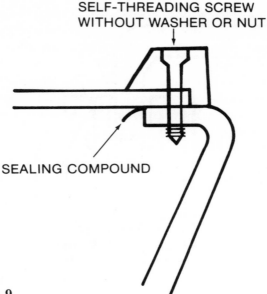

SELF-THREADING SCREW
WITHOUT WASHER OR NUT

SEALING COMPOUND

Figure 9

water valves you probably have on your house. They have a
circular handle and require several turns to open or close fully.
Sea cocks, on the other hand, have a lever which only has to be
moved 90 degrees from full on to full off. This means they can
be closed more quickly than a gate valve and, since it is a good
idea to close the through hulls—except the cockpit drains, of
course—when leaving the boat, sea cocks are closed more con-
veniently. However, they can more easily be opened by accident.

On the other hand, gate valves are manufactured in the
millions for many uses while sea cocks are made only in the
hundreds for yachts. Sea cocks are much more expensive than
gate valves, and I see no objection to gate valves so long as they
are bronze, not brass, and are properly mounted. Sea cocks
also are subject to being closed by vibrations set up by the
engine, and so some manufacturers have taken the wise step of
using gate valves at the cockpit drains and engine-water intake
and sea cocks elsewhere.

Most sailors tend to look the other way when the subject of engines comes up. I must admit I don't understand them fully. I have found, though, that by adopting a god-slave relationship with the engine (it the god, I the slave) and offering up regular sacrifices of fresh spark plugs and clean oil, we are able to live on the same boat and carry out our respective duties. To facilitate this relationship, good access to the engine is required. And this is definitely something to check.

Normally, the engine is tucked away under the cockpit and is reached via the seat lockers and/or removal of the companionway ladder. In some boats, the engine is in the main cabin under a seat; this is terrific for accessibility but means a somewhat noisier cabin when under power.

This is just one of the many trade offs involved in any boat. You probably can't have a proper engine room in any sailboat less than 40 feet and even then only if it has a center cockpit. So the thing to do is see if normal servicing can be done without dismantling the entire galley. Also see if the engine beds look reasonably solid and note whether the installation looks neat or resembles a rat's maze.

While you are looking around for a new boat, you are going to be faced with a lot of opinion, advice, sales pitches and a certain amount of bull. The purpose of this chapter has been to show you that you don't have to rely entirely on others in selecting a boat.

By looking at certain specific real things, comparing, asking questions and using your head, you can come to solid, rational conclusions about any specific boat that interests you. Also, if you show some knowledge, it can discourage some of the baloney.

6

Buying a New Boat Step by Step

In Chapter Nine you will read about how the Smiths bought a boat. It has always seemed to me that they went about finding a boat in a good way. They had a size and price range in mind when they started. Of course, it turned out they wanted more in a boat than the initial size would allow. But they did start with something definite in mind to give their search direction.

So take some sort of starting point yourself, either size or cost, and start visiting the places where boats are on display. In the New York area, all the boat dealers advertise in the sports section of the Sunday *New York Times*. Initially, it might be best to look for a dealer who seems to have more than one boat to look at, since you should try to see as much as you reasonably can to give yourself as wide a range of choice as possible. Browse around and at first don't get too deeply involved in the process outlined in this chapter.

Like a person, a boat is an amalgam of many different

characteristics. Find several boats that appeal to you for whatever reason and *then* run through the evaluation process of Chapter 5. You will probably then be able to narrow the choice down to two or three boats. At this juncture you will have a general idea of the price of the boats. The thing to do next is to sit down and price the boats with the same equipment (suggestions on this are in the next chapter).

Let's say you have finally come down to a choice between two boats, A and B. Here is how a detailed comparison between them might look:

	Boat A	Boat B
Length overall	25'2"	26'1"
Load waterline length	19'9"	21'9"
Draft	4'1"	4'3"
Beam	8'8"	8'8"
Displacement	3400#	5400#
Sail area	256 sq. ft.	320 sq. ft.
Retail base price	$8,900.00	$7,900.00
4" thick mattress	std.	163.00
Jib halyard winch	std.	130.00
Running lights	std.	260.00
Interior lights	std.	std.
Handrails	90.00	std.
Bow pulpit	125.00	125.00
Lifelines	275.00	305.00
Sheet winches	std.	84.00
Genoa gear	std.	88.00
Head	225.00	205.00
Boot top and bottom paint	175.00	111.00
Cradle	225.00	255.00
Freight, commissioning	925.00	535.00
	$10,940.00	$10,161.00
Three sails, sail cover	945.00	1,163.00
	$11,885.00	$11,324.00

Now, at this point you have satisfied yourself that the two boats are pretty nearly equal, so far as fundamental structure goes. Thus, on the face of it, you might immediately pick Boat B because it will offer you close to a $600 savings. You figure this $600 will cover the cost of the additional items you are going to need — such things as an anchor, a stove, fire extinguishers, boarding ladder, life preservers, and the like.

You know, however, that Boat B has an iron keel, whereas A has a lead keel. At the current prices of lead, the keel in A is worth about $300 more than the cast iron in B. So the difference in price has shrunk to about half. Not much, when you are going to be investing $12,000. Additionally, Boat A has natural teak-surfaced bulkheads while B uses a teak-grained Formica, which is cheaper and, while quite nice, it's not as nice as the real thing. Figuring that the teak is probably worth $200 more than the Formica, the price differential is insignificant. How are you going to choose? Well, consider these factors.

Boat B is 2 feet longer at the waterline than A. As you will see in Part 2, this means that B has a higher speed potential. In 8 to 12 knots of breeze, B should travel at about 4.6 knots and A at about 4.4. This may not sound too significant, but in ten hours of sailing it would put B about a half hour ahead of A. The difference would be slightly greater as the wind blew harder and less as the wind decreased.

The assumption is being made here that these two are similar types and, in my example, they are. Both are modern, light displacement boats with fin keels and freestanding spade rudders. Additionally, B is a solid ton heavier than A and so would have an easier motion in a seaway and be more comfortable to be on.

An interesting test can be made at this point by dividing the weight of each boat into its total cost. For Boat A this gives a cost per pound of $3.50 and, for Boat B, $2.10. Boat A is therefore 65 percent more expensive per pound than B. Now what do you do?

Well, if you've already decided that the boats are equal

structurally and what you want is the most boat for the money, B is your choice. You could equally well decide, though, that you like the better interior finish and generally better detailing on A and figure you would rather have the smaller, "nicer" boat. The point is that you can now make a rational choice based on concrete aspects of the two boats, aspects which you have evaluated using your own eyes, hands and judgment.

My personal choice, by the way, would have been the larger, heavier Boat B. But I would surely understand anyone who decided on A. The point is that you need to analyze a boat down to the point that you can decide what it is specifically you are buying. In this case, it came down to a choice between interiors in what were, basically, equally well-made boats.

The trade off was between a larger, plainer boat and a smaller, more nicely appointed boat. The cost-per-pound analysis helped to reveal this basic fact. As the man says, there is no free lunch — you get what you pay for, and the techniques of chapter 5 plus the cost-per-pound help reveal what it is you are paying for. If the choice was A, you were paying for the interior; if B, the greater size of the boat.

So far we have been talking mainly about new boats in and of themselves, but boats are not built in a vacuum nor are they sold in one. In order to look at boats, you have to go to a place where they are on display — the boat dealer's place of business, which is normally at a boat yard.

Many people do not realize this, but the boats that are on display are not there on consignment from the builder. They belong to the dealer and have been paid for by him, either directly out of pocket or by what is called "floor planning." This is an arrangement with a bank or other financial institution in which the dealer puts up 10 percent or so of the required cash, the bank puts up the rest and the dealer pays interest and repays the bank as the boats are sold. Fair amounts of money are involved in this. A dealer with three major lines may need to stock twenty-four separate boats in order to display one of each model manufactured by the three separate companies. This can easily run to a half million dollars.

I am making a point of this because it is another factor you may want to consider. You are going to be expected to leave a substantial sum of money with the dealer when you order your boat, and you may feel more confident when you do this if you can see some evidence of financial solidity on his part. Another obvious test of this nature is to find out how long the particular dealer has been in business at that spot.

Now, while you have been looking and browsing, you will have been talking to a salesman or woman who is generally called a broker in the boat business. Brokers are commissioned sales people. In other words he is paid when he closes a sale. You will find, I think, that a knowledgeable broker can be a big help to you in the buying process because he can answer many questions and often suggest alternatives that you might not have considered. Basically, a good broker will try to find (from among the boats he sells) the one he feels best fits your tastes and needs and then show you why.

Once you have found the boat you want, you will have the choice of either buying the boat on display, if it is unsold, or ordering a boat like it to be made for you. In either case, once you have reached this point there are certain, specific things that have to be done.

First, you will sit down with the broker and decide on the specifics of your boat—color, equipment, size of winches and other details. These things will be written out on a sales agreement or contract to be signed by you and an officer of the company.

At this point, a check for 10 to 15 percent of the purchase is normally required from you. After you have written it, you have completed the process of ordering a new boat.

Now there will be a lapse of time of weeks or months until the boat is completed by the factory. When your boat is completed, it is normally shipped by truck to the dealer who then will launch, rig and commission it. Once again, your boat is not shipped to the dealer on consignment. The dealer must pay for it before it is unloaded from the truck. Therefore, you will be expected to pay the dealer very soon after the arrival of the boat, and this is usually stipulated quite plainly in the sales agreement.

At this point, it might be a good idea to look at a typical sales agreement. The front is filled out to reflect your purchase of Boat A; the back, reproduced on pages 64 and 65, is fairly standard in its conditions.

The agreement should specify a month of completion, since a good builder will normally meet these dates within five to ten days. Nevertheless, early ordering is a good idea and in our area (northeast U.S.), most auxiliaries ordered for spring delivery are ordered by Thanksgiving. Remember that even the largest builders can build no more than about six hundred boats a year.

You may have noticed the area at the bottom of the contract where it says "trade." Many people are not aware they can use their present boat as part payment for their new boat. In fact, some dealers will not take trades because of the financial risks involved.

You see, if a dealer takes your boat in trade and has not sold it by the time your new boat arrives, he has to come up with whatever amount of cash he has allowed you in order to pay the manufacturer for the new boat. Some dealers do take trades; the advantages to you are often considerable.

The biggest advantage is the fact that sales tax is figured on the difference between the price of the new boat and the amount allowed for the trade. Thus, if you were buying a $20,000 new boat and your trade was valued at $10,000, instead of paying, say, 5 percent of $20,000, or $1,000, in sales tax, you would only pay $500, thus saving $500.

Additionally, if you don't have the time or inclination to find a buyer for your boat, you aren't going to have to pay a broker to find one for you. The company that takes your boat

SALES AGREEMENT

SOLD TO: John G. Smythe

92 Hickory Grove

Larchmont, NY   ZIP 10538

PHONE/HOME _____ OFFICE _____

DATE OF ORDER 10-21-75

SCHEDULED COMPLETION DATE March '76

YACHT BROKER HHS

INVENTORY NO. 2033   HULL NO. 171

1976 Pandora 25 with standard equipment per brochure	$8,900.00
Interior handrails	90.00
Bow pulpit	125.00
Life lines	275.00
Marine toilet	225.00
Boot top: red Bottom paint: blue	175.00
Shipping and Storage Cradle	225.00
Commissioning	325.00
3 sails and mainsail cover (red)	945.00

TRADE DESCRIPTION					
				SUB TOTAL	$11,285.00
MAKE & MODEL	YEAR	L.O.A.	HULL #		
				SUB TOTAL	$11,285.00
ENGINE MAKE & HP	YEAR	LISTING #	DETAILS ATTACHED YES☐ NO☐	SALES TAX(Rate)	564.00
				FREIGHT	600.00
PAYMENT SCHEDULE				TOTAL	12,449.00
BALANCE IS DUE AND PAYABLE WHEN BOAT ARRIVES IN SELLER'S YARD AT				* PAID ON ACCOUNT	2,449.00
WHICH TIME PURCHASER IS REQUIRED TO INSURE HIS INTEREST. ALL CLOSING FUNDS SHALL BE IN CASH OR BANK CHECK.				BALANCE TO BE PAID	$10,000.00

THE GENERAL CONDITIONS ENUMERATED ON THE REVERSE SIDE OF THIS FORM ARE HEREBY MADE A PART OF THIS AGREEMENT. PURCHASER ACKNOWLEDGES RECEIPT OF COPY OF THIS AGREEMENT AND AGREES TO ITS PROVISIONS.

ABC NEW BOAT CORPORATION: SELLER

X _____

VALID ONLY IF SIGNED BY PRESIDENT OR TREASURER.   SIGNATURE OF PURCHASER

in trade will have to do that. In those parts of the country where boating is seasonal, if you trade your boat at the end of the season, you will be spared the costs of winterizing and storing the boat until the next season.

Generally speaking, the reasons for the purchase of a new, rather than a used, boat can be summed up as follows:

GENERAL CONDITIONS

1. This Sales Agreement shall be valid only as and when accepted in writing by the Seller signed by either it's President or Treasurer.

2. In the event the manufacturer of any item covered by this Sales Agreement shall increase or decrease the selling price thereof to the Seller prior to delivery to the Seller, the price of any item enumerated herein shall be increased or decreased by an amount equal to the percentage of increase or decrease on such item which the Seller shall be obligated to pay to such manufacturer. In the event, however, that the purchaser may be dissatisfied with such price change, he may, within ten days notice of such price change, cancel this order; in which event if a used boat and/or engine has been traded in as part of the consideration herein, such used boat and/or engine shall be returned to the purchaser upon the payment of a reasonable charge for storage and repairs (if any) or, if the used boat and/or engine has been previously sold by the dealer, the amount received therefor, less a selling commission of 10% and any expense incurred in storing, insuring, conditioning, or advertising said boat and/or engine for sale, shall be returned to the purchaser.

3. Upon the failure or refusal of the purchaser to complete said purchase within 10 days after delivery by builder and notification to the purchaser, for any reason other than cancellation on account of increase in price, the cash deposit may be retained as liquidated damages; and in the event a used boat and/or engine has been taken in trade, the purchaser hereby authorizes the Seller to sell said used boat and/or engine; and the dealer shall be entitled to reimburse himself out of the proceeds of such sale, for the expenses specified in paragraph 2 above and also for his expenses and losses incurred or suffered as the result of purchaser's failure to complete said purchase.

4. The manufacturer has the right to make any changes in the model or design of any accessories and part of any new boat and/or engine at any time without creating obligation on the part of either the Seller or the Manufacturer to make corresponding changes in the boat and/or engine covered by this Sales Agreement either before or subsequent to the delivery of such boat and/or engine to the purchaser.

5. The Seller shall not be liable for any delay or default due to: Acts of God, delays in transportation, inability or delay of manufacturer, supplier or seller to obtain necessary labor, material or equipment to complete delivery of boat in proper working condition; strikes, fires, floods, accidents or other causes beyond the control of the Seller.

6. The price of the boat and/or engine quoted herein does not include any tax or taxes imposed by any governmental authority prior to or at the time of

delivery of such boat and/or engine **unless expressly so stated,** but the purchaser assumes and agrees to pay, unless prohibited by law any taxes, except income taxes, imposed on or incidental to the transaction herein, regardless of the person having the primary tax liability.

7. The Seller has made no representations nor makes any representations, express or implied, regarding the equipment covered by this order, except that the Seller will deliver to the Purchaser good title to said equipment free from all liens and encumbrances. Warranties by Manufacturers of the equipment covered by this order are limited to such written warranties as may accompany the individual items of equipment ordered hereunder. In all events, the Seller's warranty is limited to an obligation, subject to performance by the manufacturer of such equipment, to repair or replace any item of equipment sold hereunder, at Seller's own expense, which proves to be defective in workmanship or material, only to the limits set by the written Manufacturer's warranty. No officer or other representative or agent of the Seller is authorized to assume any other liability or obligation in connection with the sale of the equipment or materials covered by this order, and no other liability or obligation may be assumed.

8. In case the boat and/or engine covered by this Sales Agreement is a used boat and/or engine, no warranty or representation is made regarding said used boat and/or engine, it being sold "as is" in its present condition.

9. Title to the goods or boat(s) covered by this Sales Agreement shall remain in the Seller until all sums due and to become due hereunder shall be fully paid in cash by the Buyer.

10. This agreement may not be changed orally in any respect and contains the full and complete understanding between the Seller and the Purchaser regarding the purchase, sale and delivery of the equipment enumerated herein.

1. The boat may be a new model not previously available.

2. You can have the boat the way *you* want it in terms of equipment, colors and so forth.

3. Everything is brand-new and at its greatest strength and longest useful life.

4. The problem of what to do with your present boat can be solved.

5. You get warranty protection.

6. Because there is a warranty, any problems can be expected to be taken care of by the builder.

In connection with this last point, here is the wording of a fairly typical warranty certificate issued by (in my opinion) one of the better manufacturers of stock, fiberglass, auxiliary sailboats.

The most important thing to know about a warranty is who is going to carry out the work if any is needed under the terms of the warranty. It is important for you to find out if the dealer you are buying from has a boat yard which is directly under his control or if he simply "farms out" any service work.

Obviously, if he has his own yard, you as a customer have much more clout. This also holds true for the commissioning (making ready) of your boat when it arrives from the factory. Ask the broker about these things and, when you leave the sales office, take a look around outside to see if there is indeed a waterfront and whether or not the operation looks well-run or otherwise.

Again, these are not absolutes. Compare as you go from dealer to dealer. Use your eyes and common sense. Find out if there is a year-round, full-time employee solely responsible for yard operations or if the operation is strictly seasonal: you may want something done on your boat in the middle of winter.

XYZ YACHTS
Limited Warranty

1. What is Covered and for How Long:

XYZ Yachts warrants all boats and parts manufactured by it to be free from defects in material and workmanship under normal use and circumstances and with normal care and maintenance for a period of 12 months from the date of delivery to the original consumer.

2. What is not Covered:

This warranty does not apply to:

(a) Paints, varnishes, gelcoats, chrome plated or anodized finishes and other surface coatings.

(b) All installed equipment and accessories not manufactured by XYZ, including but not limited to engines, pumps, batteries, heating, refrigeration and plumbing equipment, and stereo equipment.

Where possible, however, all warranties furnished by these component part manufacturers will be passed on to the consumer.

3. Under What Circumstances Will the Warranty not Apply:

There will be no warranties whatever:

(a) Where the boat is altered or repaired by persons unauthorized by XYZ.

(b) Where a hydraulic backstay adjuster is installed.

(c) Where rigging changes are made unless first approved in writing by XYZ or made at the XYZ factory.

4. Where and How are Warranty Claims Made:

All warranty claim notifications must be made through an authorized XYZ dealer within 30 days after discovery of the defect. An inspection may be made within a reasonable time by an authorized representative after receipt of the claim notification. When a warranty claim is valid, XYZ or its authorized representative shall have the option of either replacing and installing, or having installed, the defective component part, or requiring that the part be returned for repair or replacement to XYZ. Claims for reimbursement, if any, must be submitted upon their completion on the standard XYZ Warranty Service Claim form, available either from the dealer or XYZ Yachts.

5. Limitation on the Length of Implied Warranties:

THE IMPLIED WARRANTIES OF MERCHANTABILITY AND/OR FITNESS FOR A PARTICULAR PURPOSE ARE LIMITED IN DURATION TO THE PERIOD OF 12 MONTHS FROM THE DATE OF DELIVERY TO THE ORIGINAL CONSUMER.

6. Other Important Information:

(a) XYZ DOES NOT, UNDER ANY CIRCUMSTANCES, ASSUME RESPONSIBILITY FOR THE LOSS OF TIME, INCONVENIENCE OR OTHER CONSEQUENTIAL DAMAGES, INCLUDING BUT NOT LIMITED TO, EXPENSES FOR TRANSPORTATION AND TRAVEL, TELEPHONE, LODGING, LOSS OR DAMAGE TO PERSONAL PROPERTY OR LOSS OF REVENUE.

(b) Cracks in finishes which might appear at the hull-to-keel ballast joint are normal and should not be considered as evidence of defective workmanship or material.

(c) Leaks at stanchions and chain plates resulting from day to day operation of the boat are normal and considered part of consumer maintenance.

(d) XYZ reserves the right to make changes in the design and material of its boats and component parts without incurring any obligations to incorporate such changes in units already completed or in the hands of Dealers or consumers.

(e) The entire obligation of XYZ regarding the sale or rental of its boats is stated within this written warranty. XYZ does not authorize its Dealers or any other person to assume for it any other liability in connection with the sale or rental of its boats.

(f) Section 15 of the Federal Boat Safety Act requires boat manufacturers to obtain certain data from the purchasers of its products. We cannot fulfill our obligation under this important Act without your cooperation. Would you, therefore, please complete the Warranty Registration Certificate accompanying this warranty and return it to us as soon as possible. If you need assistance in completing the card, please check with your XYZ Dealer or contact us directly and we will be glad to assist you.

In 1975 the U.S. Congress passed a law to help consumers — all consumers, even the boat buyer. It is known officially as the Consumer Product Warranties Law, although it is also known by the name Magnuson-Moss Warranty Act, after the men who sponsored it. Its purpose is to regulate consumer product warranty practices; thus, it applies almost exclusively to new boats. The Federal Trade Commission has the responsibility for enacting rules under the law and enforcing compliance. Its first rules were issued at the end of 1975 and became effective during 1976. Manufacturers and dealers are already reacting to the new requirements.

As we are all aware, manufacturers have utilized many different varieties of warranties over the years, some good and some bad. Some were so complicated that consumers couldn't understand them, some required specific affirmative behavior by the consumer to avoid forfeiture of his rights, others just started out worthless.

Reputable manufacturers usually gave fair warranties and

honored them. Others wrote beautiful warranties and never intended to honor them; the warranty was simply a sales tool. The new law hopes to end the abuses.

However, its requirements are strict and could cause even the best manufacturers to cut back on their warranties. If that happens, at least you'll know before you buy that your new boat has a weak warranty. Of course, if something not covered occurs, the reputable builder may fix it free anyway if it's clearly his fault, but the decision will be entirely his, not yours.

Here are details. There will be two basic types of warranties, those called "full" and those called "limited." A written warranty must be either one or the other. The designation should appear prominently as a title, set apart from any text at the top of the warranty document. Most warranties will be limited, because a full warranty must meet tough minimum standards under the law. It's also possible for a complex product like a boat to carry both full and limited warranties, each applicable to different features of the boat.

Basically, under a full warranty, the manufacturer must promptly repair or, if that isn't feasible, replace any item covered. All the consumer has to do is notify the manufacturer, as the warranty must tell him how to. There can be no charge to the buyer.

The warranty must state its duration, which must be "reasonable," taking into account the nature of the product. In addition, using reasonableness as a guide, a full warranty has a provision to force replacement or even refund of a "lemon." One reason why manufacturers will probably avoid issuing full warranties is that there can be no limitation of the duration of an "implied warranty" under a full warranty.

An implied warranty, for those of you who didn't bother to become lawyers, is based essentially on the assumption that a product is suitable for the purpose for which it is sold. For instance, regardless of whether or not you get a written warranty—or even a promise from a salesman—there is an implied warranty that your new boat will float, that it won't leak huge quantities of water through its deck, and that its chain plates won't pull out under normal use in a light breeze.

But, because sooner or later anything wears out, a manufacturer isn't unreasonable if he issues a limited warranty, because he then can limit the duration of any implied warranties to the duration of the limited warranty. That duration, though, must be reasonable.

The new law requires that a limited warranty clearly spell out what is covered and what is not. The manufacturer, however, cannot disclaim basic implied warranties, for a provision restricts limitations to those which are "conscionable." (There will probably be a lot of heated discussion over what that means, once problems occur.)

All warranties must be made available to you to read before you commit to buy. This right can be of great value to you if you take advantage of it. Read and compare warranties, just as you compare any other feature of the boat. You'll get a good idea of which builders talk straight and want to be fair and which ones are concerned only about selling. You'll also have a standard against which to measure your salesman's sales pitch.

If there's an inconsistency, believe the warranty, although, as I mentioned above, the good manufacturers (encouraged by ethical dealers) in extreme situations may do what's right regardless of any warranty.

7

Equipping a New Boat

Six or seven years ago, the boating industry was locked in the battle of the "base price." Manufacturers strove to be able to put the lowest possible price in their ads, and so they left more and more things off the boat and put them instead on so-called "option" sheets. Would you believe that at the 1970 New York Boat Show was a 38-foot sailboat for which the engine was optional?

Fortunately, boat buyers have become more sophisticated and the trend now is definitely away from this sort of thing. Several manufacturers are now offering boats with equipment so complete that it is necessary only to truck the boat from the factory, launch it, rig it, add sails (not supplied by the boat builder — and a good thing, too) in order to sail away.

One of the difficulties today is that most everyone has a slightly different idea of what constitutes "proper" equipment for a boat. Remember, one of the advantages of buying a new boat is that you get to equip it the way you want, to your tastes and prejudices — not anyone else's.

To avoid getting tangled up in endless debate, what I propose to do is to suggest to you what I consider the proper level of equipment for any given size of boat, based upon the prime consideration that you will not keep the boat more than half the length of time that you think. Since you'll undoubtedly be moving up sooner than you think, my suggestions are made with an eye to the resale market.

In other words, the following equipment guide is made with an eye to making your boat as appealing as possible to the used-boat buyer or dealer who is going to have to take her in trade. What I am suggesting is an equipping guide that will maximize the amount of dollars returned to you from the investment originally made in your boat.

22′ to 28′ Outboard Powered

Two-tone deck
Bow pulpit, lifelines, stern rail
Main and jib halyard winches
Jiffy reefing gear
Genoa gear
Large, single-speed Genoa sheet winches
6 (22′), 10 (26′), 15 (28′) HP motor
Boarding ladder
Lightning-grounded rigging, thru-hulls
Interior, running lights
Interior, exterior handrails
Head
Cradle
Galley with sink, stove
Main, jib, Genoa, mainsail covers
Coast Guard-required equipment

Many of these things will be standard from the better builders, especially such an item as grounded rigging to protect you from the effects of a lightning strike. Items such as depth finders, ship-to-shore radios and speedometers will not return their investment in this size range of boats. A boat over 28′ with an outboard motor is a joke on the used market.

27′ to 31′ Inboard Powered

Bow pulpit, lifelines, stern rail
Lifeline gate starboard side
Main and jib halyard winches
Genoa gear
2-speed genoa sheet winches
2 batteries with cross-over switch
Universal Atomic 4 or equivalent inboard engine
All required safety gear
Boarding ladder
Lightning-grounded rigging, hulls
Interior, running lights
Interior, exterior handrails
Head
Cradle
Sink in the head
Galley with two-burner, flush-mounted stove
Main, jib, Genoa, mainsail covers
Jiffy reefing gear
Speedometer, depth finder, ship-to-shore, RDF

At this size boat, steering wheels start to become attractive, as do diesel engines. But, for purposes of resale, you should consider half the funds invested in either of these two items as gone for good.

32′ to 35′

Everything on the above list. If you can swing it, a diesel installed now will probably pay off three years from now. Today, it's still pretty much 50-50 so far as the market is concerned. But the trend is to diesel. Now, for the other equipment:

Wheel with brake, guard, throttle
Emergency tiller

Double lifelines
Mainsheet winch
Dodger
2 anchors
H/C pressure water and shower
Briquet-burning cabin heater
3-burner Gimballed stove with oven

36′ to 42′:

Everything above
Diesel is a must
Storm trysail and storm jib
Log (records elapsed miles, like odometer on car)
2-speed jib halyard winch
2-speed mainsheet winch

Somewhere around 34′ a split rig (yawl or ketch) becomes desirable from the point of view of eventual resale in a cruising boat.

The rational reason for installing a pedestal steering wheel on a boat is simply for the mechanical advantage. Once a boat reaches around five tons displacement, the forces generated at the rudder are quite large and steering with a tiller becomes very tiring. In smaller boats (27 to 32 feet), the wheel will cancel out the torque effect of the propeller; this makes the boat want to turn in one direction when under power. A pedestal wheel will make it possible for even small children to steer while under power.

In addition to these rational reasons, there is the irrational fact that a wheel is a real ego-booster for most people. It just looks and feels "right." On an outboard-powered boat, however, a wheel is a joke and your sailing friends will be embarrassed to know you. So if you want a wheel, get inboard power for sure.

The principal reason to have a diesel engine is the safety factor. Its fuel is like the heating oil used in your furnace at home; if some were to leak into the bilge of your boat, it's merely messy, but not as dangerous as gasoline. Gasoline in the bilge, on the other hand, forms an explosive mixture with air that can go off at the tiniest spark.

In choosing between gasoline or diesel for boats under 35 feet, however, there is a trade off: small diesels often run more noisily and produce more vibration than a gasoline engine. This is because the diesels suitable for small boats are usually one or two cylinders, and so the firing pattern cannot be overlapped to promote smoothness the way it can with a 4-cylinder gasoline engine. The larger diesels with four or more cylinders are very smooth running and no noisier than the equivalent-horsepower gasoline engine.

To put this into some perspective, let me say that in the twenty years of sailing I did prior to going into the business, I never met anyone who had a gasoline explosion on a sailboat. I did see two large powerboats explode (with no serious injuries).

In the seven years I have been selling boats, I have met two people who had gasoline explosions on their sailboats. But I've met five people whose boats have been struck by lightning.

In thinking about this, I have come up with the following: powerboats commonly have two large engines fueled from large tanks; the boats are pushed through the water at speeds two to four times those at which sailboats move. As a result, the vibration and shocks are many times greater. This means that fuel lines are more likely to loosen or break with the resulting leakage and fume buildup.

My basic feeling, therefore, is that on a boat up to 32 feet that is going to be used along shore or within a sound or lake, a gasoline engine is fine. Any boat, though, that is going offshore out of sight of land should have a diesel. At this point, safety becomes the paramount consideration, and the greater cost of the diesel has to be considered in the category of safety equipment.

8

Check List for New Boats

This is an attempt to pull together in one place the divers elements that go into the final evaluation of a boat. The list is applicable to used boats as well as new although, obviously, some deterioration in exterior finish, rig, engine, and sails is to be expected in a used boat. The presumption is made that before using this list you have found one or more boats that appeal to you that you want to make a comparative evaluation. I am also assuming that you are satisfied with the quality of the boats produced by the company from which you are planning to buy.

Exterior

1. Gel-coat like:
   —A new billiard ball
   —An orange peel
2. Hard spots (creases) showing where bulkheads are:
   —None

    —Few

    —A lot

3. Hull sweeps in smooth curves from bow to stern:
   —No flat spots
   —A few flat spots
   —Many flat spots
4. Very faint print-through of roving if at all.
5. Rudder post substantial (compare one boat to another if same type; spade, spade with skeg, barn door)?
6. Attachment of ballast to hull shows careful work?
7. Cockpit seat lockers sturdy?
8. Good waterways around lockers?
9. Substantial hinges on lockers?
10. Side decks wide enough to allow easy access to fore-deck and mast?
11. Lifelines:
    —Above knee height
    —Stanchions through-bolted with 4 bolts
    —Compare lifeline diameters
12. Chainplates:
    —Compare sizes
    —Compare manner of attachment to hull
13. Hatches:
    —Compare for relative
      —sturdiness
      —watertightness

Interior

1. Compare fundamental work by:
   —Looking in hanging locker at final layer of glass; best if it is roving, not mat
     —checking type of hull-deck joint
     —looking at smoothness of work at hull-deck joint
     —finding chain-plate buttresses and compar-

ing sizes and level of workmanship—i.e., smoothness and massiveness
- —opening lockers and (carefully) running hand over glass surfaces to see if smooth and fair or full or raw edges and "icicles" which can cut you
- —Checking engine installation for
    - —sturdiness of beds
    - —shut-off valve on water intake
    - —fuel lines carefully routed and secured with neoprene padded fastenings and aircraft flexibility tubing where required
- —Checking to see that all below-water through-hulls are fitted with bronze shut-offs properly installed with backing blocks
- —Checking wiring to see comparative gauges used and whether or not protected against chafe where it goes through bulkheads. If wiring goes through bilge area, make sure it is underwater quality
- —Checking fuel tank material

Gas	*Diesel*
Best—Monel	Monel
Very Good—Aluminum	Aluminum
Alum. coated steel	Black Iron
Zinc coated steel	Mild Steel
(galvanized steel)	
Terneplate	

- —Checking mast step area and keel bolts for comparative massiveness of materials and signs of special reinforcement to take heavy loads
- —Checking battery installation; batteries should be in acid proof plastic boxes with a lid and well strapped down

2. Compare finish work by:
- Observing fit of joints and seams
- The way drawers are made and finished
- Whether or not drawers and lockers have positive latches (best) as opposed to friction fittings
- How smoothly drawers and doors slide, engine covers remove, switches switch, etc.

At the Factory
- Size of plant
- General level of orderliness and cleanliness
- Level of activity—i.e., are they really building boats or just stooging around
- This is one place you can really see the boat totally, so look at:
    - hull thickness at various points
    - secondary bonding
    - exact manner of joining hull and deck
    - engine and tank installations
    - wiring installation
    - insulation of ice boxes

- If you are not going to be able to get to the factory and want to check the thickness of the hull, have a through-hull fitting withdrawn on a display model of the boat you are considering.

At Home

Cost of boat per pound in the water with equipment you want on her.

Final Note

Bear in mind that this list is to be used on a comparative basis not on an absolute basis. I am not trying to make you into structural engineers, but if you look at certain specific things on two or three different boats, a picture will emerge showing which boat is likely to be strongest. Like anything else in life, boats are a mixture of good and bad features and your final choice is inevitably going to be a compromise — a compromise, though, illuminated by your knowledge. Not until there are perfect people will there be perfect boats and if, after all your comparing and checking, you find yourself still in love with a boat that doesn't seem to measure up, consider having her surveyed when completed at the factory.

9

Case History

Six years ago Mr. and Mrs. Charles Smith came into our office. They had been sailing in rented daysailers for a few years and were now considering the purchase of a small cruising boat. Their feeling was that a 26-footer would be about right for them.

On the way out to the showroom to look at boats in this size range, Mr. Smith asked how much a 26-footer was likely to cost. "By the time you have her completely equipped," I replied, "about $9,000." Mr. and Mrs. Smith halted with stricken looks on their faces. Good heaven, they thought you could buy a boat of this size for about $5,000 complete!

I told them they could get into a 22-footer for about $5,000, but they had been sailing 22-footers and knew they were just too small for their requirements. I suggested that we take a look at the 25- and 26-footers in the showroom, and we proceeded to do this.

When we got on the first boat, Mr. Smith was very interested in the way the boat was built, how well she sailed and other more or less technical aspects of the boat.

The first question Mrs. Smith asked, however, was if a shower could be installed—and couldn't the head be put to one side so there would be complete privacy for using the head and for the forward berths?

I explained that there was only so much the designers could do with the cubic feet available in a 26-footer, and that the arrangement we were looking at was the most practical for this size boat.

Further, I pointed out that there was no way to heat water for a shower system on this boat. That required an inboard engine with a heat exchanger, and boats with inboards cost a lot more than boats powered with outboards.

At this point, Mr. and Mrs. Smith were getting a little frustrated, so to clear the air a little I suggested we look at a used boat that I figured was within reasonable range of their intended budget, and we went outside to look at it.

Now, this particular used boat was a year-old model of the new one in the showroom. In my opinion, it was as clean as a new coin and, if anything, more appealing than the new one because of some personal touches added by the owner—such things as a brass clock and barometer on one bulkhead and a handsome kerosene lamp on the other.

Mrs. Smith, however, noticed some minute amounts of dust in the corners of the shelves, a little mildew in the hanging locker and rust rings from beer cans in the bottom of the icebox, and it became very obvious to me that Mrs. Smith was never going to buy a used boat. Back to the showroom.

This time I decided to go for broke. I got them onto a 35-footer that had all the things Mrs. Smith wanted: a truly private head with shower, a door for the forward cabin, a large stove with oven. This was the boat for Mrs. Smith, all right! She lighted up and couldn't stop talking. Obviously this was what she had had in mind all the time, but, being unused to the scale of boats, she had thought the amenities she wanted could be had in a very small boat.

Mr. Smith was also enthusiastic about the boat. He particularly liked the steering wheel and the diesel engine. I could tell, however, that he was wondering what all this would cost. Before we went into that, I suggested that we look at some boats in the 30- to 33-foot range to see if any of them would suit the Smiths. Not one did. That 35-footer had all they wanted in a boat.

Mr. Smith now asked the price of the 35-footer, and now it was my turn to be surprised. Instead of turning pale at the figure (about six times what they were initially figuring on investing), Mr. Smith simply asked me if I thought he could handle such a big boat.

I told him I was sure he could. I pointed out that, although the 35 weighed nearly three times as much as the 26, she didn't have even twice the sail area and the winches were three times as powerful. So sail handling would be relatively easier. With the inboard engine and wheel, manuevering under power would also be easier. I suggested that he talk with some friends who had boats of around 35 feet and see what they thought.

Mr. Smith did this, and then he and his wife spent about a month looking at other makes of boats before finally settling on one of our 35-footers. Mrs. Smith was particularly happy because she got to choose a particularly lovely hull color for their new boat.

I have told this story because it has been replayed many times at our office and has resulted in an often-repeated piece of advice (a sales pitch, if you will): buy as big a boat as you can, right off the bat. There are many cogent reasons for this, and some of them arise from the basic physical laws discussed in Part 2 of this book—i.e., in any given weather or sea condition, a large boat is more stable, drier and altogether more comfortable than a small one.

Up to 40 feet, a sailboat is easily within the competence of any adult who knows his limitations and exercises common sense. Indeed, I, having been taught to sail by the make-a-mistake-and-you-capsize method, am frankly amazed at the high degree of competence that raw newcomers acquire and the speed with which they acquire it. It's all a question of motivation.

To return to Mr. Smith for a moment, there is another aspect of buying big to begin with, and that is financial. As you know, inflation is not likely to go away. So, not only has Mr. Smith not had to go through the (expensive) process of trading up every two years, but the replacement cost of his boat is now such (about 50 percent more than he paid) that his boat on the used market would return him more dollars than he originally invested. There are many people who haven't done that well in the stock market in the past six years.

With their boat the Smiths have had a lot of fun and some adventures, gone places in a peaceful and normal manner, entertained — and, yes, impressed — their friends. To top it all, their investment is secure and will be there when they want it returned in cash.

10

Self-Steering

To me, the most boring job on a sailboat is steering. I have found that, after about 20 minutes or so, I get tired of having to sit and basically do nothing. After all, if the sails are properly trimmed for the course, steering consists of making very minor movements of the wheel or tiller—very nearly doing nothing.

My idea of the way to go sailing is to get the boat on course, adjust the sails and centerboard, if the boat has one, and then to walk away from the helm and, while keeping a good lookout, to putter about the boat doing the multitude of little jobs that always need doing in any sailboat. My very favorite thing is to sit in the cockpit with a cup of tea or a beer and just watch the world go by as the boat slides along, steering herself.

Now, to achieve the above idyll requires (1) that the boat be fitted with either an auto-pilot which uses electricity and steers the boat to a compass heading by means of a built-in compass or (2) that the boat be fitted with what is called a wind vane self-steerer. This device steers the boat at a constant, predetermined angle to the wind. It is not usable when the boat is under power and so is more limited in usefulness than an autopilot, which can steer under either wind or power.

On the other hand, a well-engineered and constructed wind vane steerer is simpler and more rugged, and it does not draw power from the ship's batteries. So it is the preferred method of auto-helming used by long-distance sailors and serious, coast-wise cruisers.

The only objection I can see to the wind vane self-steerers is that they are usually not very pretty and, since they have to be mounted at the stern of the boat, do not always enhance her looks. Thought is being given to this aspect of the vane gear, and there are several models now on the market that are noticeable improvements over the early stuff, which was usually amateurishly built and very spindly looking.

As with most other things about boats, vane gear is not cheap. The unit on the 40-footer on which I regularly sail cost $700 in 1972, and the owner of the boat did the installation himself. Some of the newer and nicer-looking models now coming on the market run about $2,000. Still, if you have gotten to the point where you find steering a chore, look into these.

Further Reading

An excellent book is available on this subject. It is *Self-Steering for Sailing Craft* by John S. Letcher Jr. Camden, Maine: International Marine Publishing Co., 1974.

11

Maintaining Your Boat

In the eight years I've worked as a yacht broker, I have continually been astounded at the generally low state of maintenance of boats coming on the used market. I am astonished because had these boats been better maintained, I as a broker would have been able to get thousands of dollars more for the sellers of these boats. Since the majority of used sailboats are fiberglass these days, the low state of maintenance is also surprising because maintenance of fiberglass boats is basically a cleaning job. It is so easy to keep the boat appealing. Just keep it clean!

To go into this more specifically, the following is an idea of the maintenance program for a fiberglass auxiliary sailboat of recent vintage in an area where the boat is customarily stored, or laid up, for the winter.

In the fall, after the yard has hauled the boat and set her in her cradle, and after the engine, head and water system have been winterized:

—Strip the boat of everything movable and take it home (boat owners should have station wagons or vans).

—Send the mattress covers out to be dry-cleaned.

—Send the sails to a sailmaker for washing and have him check for, and make, any repairs needed.

—Soak in fresh water the halyards, sheets, blocks, anything else that will benefit. Dry, coil, lubricate (blocks and metal gear) and store in a clean, dry place.

—Clean up all the other gear as appropriate.

—Have the fire-extinguishers recharged if the gauge shows low pressure.

—Fill the fuel tank and add a pint of dry gas.

—Some weekend when the weather is decent, go down to the boat and thoroughly clean the inside from bow to stern. This includes the engine, under the floorboards, the bilges. Go after the stove; get the rings out of the bottom of the icebox. Before you leave the boat, open all the lockers (the drawers should have been taken home as well as the lid of the icebox). Have the yard build a frame and cover the boat and some nice weekend come down and, if the local vandalism quotient is low enough, take the swash boards out of the companionway and open the ports, hatches and seat lockers so the boat can have a good airing under her winter cover. If the mast has been taken out of the boat and is accessible, check (or have someone knowledgeable check) the shrouds, tangs and terminal fittings for wear and possible replacement. Then go home, sit by the fire, read boat-goodie catalogs and dream about the season to come.

Now, the above doesn't have to be drudgery. As a matter of fact, most people enjoy it. Many find going down to the boat yard a great way of getting out of many homeside chores that are not nearly as much fun as messing around with the boat.

In the spring, get the cover off, dismantle the frame and, starting from the top of the cabin, sand or chemically clean the exterior teak, hose the boat down and scrub the decks and cockpit. Then:

— Compound and wax the hull.

— Paint the boot top, then the bottom.

— Get the sails from the sailmaker and the covers from the cleaners if you didn't do it in the winter.

— Truck all the stuff down to the boat and reassemble the interior.

— Tell the yard to launch and rig the boat and commission the engine.

During the season, as you get the chance, hose the boat off with fresh water, including the lower mast areas and the shrouds and turnbuckles. Keep an eye on the condition of the bottom and, if it starts to get foul, either haul and clean or swim and clean. It is absolutely amazing how much effect on the speed and handling even the least amount of growth has.

Enjoy it!

12

Preparing a Stock Boat for Offshore

Recently a stock production sailboat came into our dock. She was built by one of the major builders of production boats, and what attracted my attention was the baggy-wrinkle chafing gear on her aft lower shrouds, at the places where a mainsail might rub when the mainsail was well out, as on a broad reach or run.

Normally, inshore cruisers don't use this chafe-preventing gear because the boat does not sail for lengthy periods on any one point of sail. Offshore boats, however, often do, and I wondered if this boat had, perhaps, spent any significant time offshore.

I was really intrigued because this particular model was one in which I had contemplated a trip to Bermuda with my family; I had put my plans aside when we decided to purchase a house. I still felt, though, that this model and most of the other boats from this manufacturer were very strongly made and capable of offshore cruising with minor modifications.

Since it appeared from the registration number painted on the bow that this boat had been sailed from Seattle to New York, I was most curious to see what modifications this person, who had done what I had only contemplated, might have made to the boat.

To my amazement, he had made very few changes. Where I would have provided shutters for the large ports in the main cabin, he had not. The companionway opening in this particular model comes to within 4 inches of the cockpit sole. A sea filling the cockpit could easily flood the cabin and seriously endanger the boat.

My plans had called for the construction of a drop-in swash board of double the thickness of the board supplied with the boat. The board would have been 1 inch thick by 18 inches high, equal to the height of the seats above the cockpit sole.

But this gent, who had actually sailed the long trip, had used the standard ½-inch by 18-inch board and had not made provision for fastening it positively in place.

Now, it did not seem that anyone could have made a trip of this length without running into bad times. And so I examined the boat carefully in the areas around the chain plates and mast step. No signs of strain. I checked the bond of the bulkheads to the hull. They appeared perfect.

What I saw was a boat pretty nearly as it had come from the factory. The serial number revealed that it was one of the first twenty of these boats built; one of the first of a boat whose numbers eventually may reach nearly 1,000, since it is still in production. The boat had been in use since 1971, and at the date I looked at it, in the spring of 1976, she was obviously wearing her age and experience with equal aplomb.

As I looked over this boat, I found that the only modifications the owner had made were additional handrails on the inside and the leading of several halyards to the cockpit so it would not be necessary to go on deck to lower the headsails in bad weather. He had also fitted a vented charcoal heater, which I am sure was a great pleasure in the typical damp and chill of Puget Sound.

As I sat and thought about this boat, I realized that, while she seemed to prove my judgment about the merits of her manufacturer, she was still some way from being prepared in a way I would feel proper for offshore sailing.

To begin with, it seems to me that, if you are going offshore, the boat has to be prepared to survive one of the ultimate tests of a boat — being rolled completely over in high seas. I have talked with people who have been through this experience and find that the things that give way in a rollover are, primarily, the hatches. You should, therefore, carefully consider all the hatches on the boat, both from the point of view of their watertightness and the possibility of a sea's catching one and tearing it right off.

The new aluminum and plexiglass hatches now appearing on many production boats seem a step in the right direction. I particularly like the ones that have an additional supporting bar down the middle and are not just a frame with a span of plexiglass à la the average window.

For the older type of fiberglass hatch, I suggest either replacement with the aluminum-plexi type or the construction of a sturdy cover that could be bolted over the hatch in the event of really severe weather.

The sliding companionway hatch on the boat from Seattle was held in place by substantial metal runners fastened to the cabin top by substantial screws fairly closely spaced. For offshore work, I would replace these screws and bolt the rail through the cabin top.

I would also replace the teak strips that held the swash boards with thick metal strips bolted through the entry way. I would cut a top swash board from 1-inch thick plexiglass and provide an inside brace to hold the companionway shut. In this way, during really severe weather the boat could be sealed and it would still be possible to see out. Come to think of it, though, in these conditions you might not want to see what was happening!

The boat from Seattle did not have shut-off valves on the cockpit drains, and I think I would install them. That way, if a hose popped loose at a bad time, an immediate fix could be applied by shutting the valve. Otherwise, a wooden plug would have to be driven into the opening; this would take more time and allow in more water than if the valve were there and ready for use.

To pass on to more fundamental considerations, it seems to me that if a boat has hull-deck joint like Figure 9 in Chapter 5, the minimum thing to do would be to withdraw the screws one by one and replace them with bolts. Before I would go to this labor, however, I would carefully consider the thickness of the hull at this point and the breadth in the turned-over edge (flange), compare it with other boats to decide whether the best course might not be to sell the boat and start from a stronger fundamental base.

I'm pretty sure I would not go offshore in a boat with a hull-deck attachment made in the manner of Figure 8. This joint has no turned-over flange to give it rigidity and, it seems to me, must work from side to side more or less violently, depending upon the state of the sea. Not only will this make the joint open and leak, it also seems to me that the rivets must eventually break or tear through the fiberglass.

Naturally, there are many, many other considerations that go into offshore sailing. But I think you must make a start with the fundamental boat, and that she must be as strong as you can realistically make her. Just to give you something to think about, imagine your boat rolled over and hanging upside down the next time you look at the engine mounts, fuel tank harness, battery tie-downs — and that Herreshoff 75-pound storm anchor you have lying in the bilge. Might be a good time to tie it down.

Further Reading

If you are intrigued by the idea of offshore sailing, I recommend the following books: *Deep Sea Sailing* by Erroll Bruce. London: Stanley Paul and Co., Ltd., 248 pages.

The Ocean Sailing Yacht by Donald Street. New York: W. W. Norton and Co., 700 pages.

Ocean Voyaging by David M. Parker. Tuckahoe, N.Y.: John de Graff, Inc., 216 pages.

13

The Manufacturer

As we already know, the boat-building industry is very small and, in dealing with the manufacturer — whether directly or through a dealer — you are not in the same position you would be in doing business with, say, Mobil Oil or United States Steel. Where you probably wouldn't feel it necessary to check the financial status of a steel or oil giant, it would be a very good idea to find out as much as you reasonably can about the manufacturers of any boats you consider seriously.

This is one of the first things our company looks into when we are approached by a builder and asked to take on his line of boats. There have been cases recently in which individuals have ordered boats, given deposits or turned in their current boat as a deposit and, come spring, found the manufacturer bankrupt. These people have lost their previous boats and/or their cash deposits.

Some boat manufacturers are publicly held corporations, and so the financial information about them is available either directly or through Dun & Bradstreet reports. Some of the builders are parts of conglomerates; the information about them may be consolidated in the annual report for the total company and not specifically segregated. Still, an inquiry into the general state of health of the parent company may give you some indication of the state of the water before you jump in.

Probably the most direct way to assess the boat builder is to visit his plant. Just the impression you receive of the general orderliness, cleanliness, size and level of activity will give you some feel for the company. It is also a good time to find out how many boats the company built last year, how many they expect to build this year and how long they have been in business continuously.

That is, it is a good time to ask if you haven't already asked the dealer or salesman you've been working with. To give you some parameters, a company that has been in business continuously for five or more years and is producing six hundred or more boats a year in the 25- to 40-foot range is likely to be stable and adequately financed. A key word here is *continuous*. There are builders who have opened and shut their doors several times in their history.

To drop this somewhat gloomy topic, a factory visit, if it's at all possible, is also a good opportunity to look into such things as the thickness of the hull, bulkheads, the strength of the engine beds and the general level of workmanship that is going into the boats.

At the factory, you will see boats in all stages of construction and many things will be visible that will vanish or be extremely difficult to view later.

To take some of those items, the fuel tank and tank beds and attachments will be visible, and it is a good time to inquire into the whys and wherefores of the tank installation and to assess whether or not the installation seems adequately strong.

If you can't tell by sight, ask what the fuel tank is made of. This is another one of the tip-offs to the real quality of the boat. Monel is the best tank material and is about ten times as expensive as any other material. A builder who is giving you a monel tank in your boat is giving you the best. A quick guide to both types of fuel tanks would look like this:

Gasoline	Diesel
Monel	Monel
Aluminum	Aluminum
Galvanized iron	Black iron
Terneplate	

The trouble with galvanized iron or terneplate tanks is that water, which is always present to some degree in the bottom of fuel tanks, eventually corrodes the tank through and the fuel gets dumped into the bilge where it is highly dangerous in the case of gasoline and very messy in the case of diesel.

Black iron is the traditional material for diesel tanks and is okay because diesel is a light oil and tends to coat the inside of the tank and protect it from corrosion.

Other areas I like to inspect when I visit a factory are wiring and plumbing. Mainly, is it neat and clear of bilge water? And, specifically, does the wiring have extra protection from chafe where it passes through the bulkhead?

All in all, a factory visit can do much either to reinforce your pleasure in your decision to buy a particular boat or make you revise your decision before it is too late. Just open your eyes, use common sense and, by all means, ask questions.

14

Documentation

Briefly, to document a boat is to register it with the federal government instead of a state government. You do this by filling out specific forms which are obtainable from the U. S. Coast Guard. The United States is divided into a number of Coast Guard districts, and you normally register your boat with the headquarters of the district in which you live.

The advantage of documenting your boat is that it gives you the clearest possible proof of ownership. This is practically a necessity if you are ever going to sail your boat to another country; its customs officers are going to want to be sure you are not in a stolen boat.

Too, when you sell the boat the buyer can be confident he has clear title because the Coast Guard maintains a file on a documented vessel and anyone who has a lien on the boat, such as the lending institution who financed the boat for you, will be on record. Thus, a buyer merely has to check with the Coast Guard to satisfy himself that he has purchased a boat free and clear.

Minor advantages of such documentation are that you do not have to clear U.S. customs if you are leaving for, say, Bermuda or the Virgin Islands. Also, you do not have to paint registration numbers on the bow of your boat, something that many people—including me—find objectionable on aesthetic grounds. No matter what you hear, documentation per se will not allow you to evade sales tax.

If you are buying a new boat, the process is fairly simple and documenting it is probably the thing to do—if the boat qualifies. Anyone lending you money to buy the boat is going to want to have the boat documented as part of the financing arrangement, for the reasons given above.

To qualify for documentation, certain of the measurements of the boat are fed into a formula. The boat can be documented if the formula produces a number of five or larger. The formula is this: overall length of the boat times its greatest beam times depth from deck to top of ballast if ballast is external (or bottom of keel if ballast is carried inside) times .0045.

This yields the theoretical internal cubic volume of the boat in hundreds of cubic feet. Thus, to qualify for documentation, the boat must have, by formula, 500 cubic feet of internal space. Each 100 of these cubic feet is called, because of tradition, a ton. A boat whose measurements when put into the formula produce a number, say, 9, is said to "measure" 9 net tons.

Now, this obviously has nothing whatever to do with the weight of the boat. These "tons" are cubic feet of air space. So do not think that if, for example, you buy a documented boat measuring 10 net tons, that she weighs 20,000 pounds. I mention this because it is a very common belief that tonnage measured and expressed in this way does represent the weight, or displacement, of the boat.

The mechanics of documentation are fairly straightforward. The builder of the boat fills out a form called the Master Carpenters Certificate. This basically states that that company built the boat and also states for whom the boat was built. In the case of a stock production boat, this will normally be for the dealer from whom you ordered the boat: you ordered the boat from the dealer and the builder constructed the boat for the dealer to sell to you. The Master Carpenter Certificate also shows the twelve-digit serial number of the boat and the measurements needed for the formula.

When you have paid for the boat, the dealer gives you two identical bills of sale on a special Coast Guard form which states, basically, that he has sold you boat Number So-and-So, as described in the Master Carpenters Certificate.

You take the Master Carpenters Certificate and the bills of sale and contact the officer in charge of the Coast Guard district in which you are going to register the boat.

You then fill out a form swearing that you are a U.S. citizen and a form in which you designate a name for the boat; a permanent unique number is assigned to your boat.

This is her number from then on. It never changes, no matter how many times she is bought or sold or in what other districts she comes to be registered as the result of those sales.

It is your responsibility to see that that number is permanently affixed to the inside of the boat. In a wood boat, this is normally done by carving the numbers into the main deck beam. In a glass boat, this is normally done by carving the number into a teak board and glassing the board into the boat.

Part 2

Instant Naval Architecture

Introduction

The purpose of Part 2 of this book is to explain in common terms the basic laws and concepts that underlie the design and performance of sailboats. Several simple experiments you can perform at home will be used to help you get a handle on these concepts. No great attempt is going to be made to get into all the finer details or ramifications of these concepts, since you are not trying to become a naval architect but simply a more knowledgeable boat buyer, looker, dreamer or whatever.

Basically, this section of the book is going to use these fundamental concepts in order to indicate answers to questions such as these: "This boat is only four feet longer than that boat; why does it cost twice as much?" and "How can a boat be tender if it has a 50 percent ballast ratio?"

As you will see, many interrelated factors are involved in the answers to these questions and many others like them; they involve hull form, speed, seaworthiness, rig, directional stability, comfort, suitability, weatherliness and so on.

1

Basic Laws

1. Displacement

Probably the most fundamental or basic thing you can know about a boat is its total weight. In naval architecture, the total weight of a boat is called its *displacement* because the weight of the boat is equal to the weight of the water that it has moved aside, or displaced, with its hull.

If you imagine a boat being slowly lowered into the water by a crane or marine railway, you can see that the hull of the boat shoves aside or displaces water. It makes a hole for itself shaped like its underbody, and, when the weight of the water trying to fill up the hole equals the weight of the boat pushing the water out of the hole, a state of equilibrium is reached—and the boat is afloat.

You can get something of a grip on this concept by taking a child's building block and slowly lowering it into a sink of water. Before the block touches the water, it has a perceptible weight. As you lower it, though, it seems to weigh less and less

111

until, finally, it has no weight you can discover and it is buoyed up by the water it has displaced.

If you were to try this experiment with a small block and a full glass of water, you would find that the amount of water that overflowed the glass would be equal in weight to the block. Similarly, if you were to lower a boat into a brimful swimming pool, the weight of the water that overflowed would equal the total weight of the boat.

Now, what is really important is not the weight or displacement of the boat per se, but its displacement in relation to its size. Thus, a 30-footer that weighs 15,000 pounds is said to be of heavy displacement (literally, a "heavyweight"), while one that displaces 5,000 pounds is said to be of light displacement, meaning it is light for its size.

To be technically and strictly correct about it, a boat's displacement should be compared to its waterline length. But, when you're looking for a boat, you are not going to think of a boat as being a boat of so many waterline feet but of so many *overall* feet.

In other words, you are going to tend to categorize boats by their total length from bow to stern and compare one boat to another in the same overall-length category rather than same waterline-length bracket.

Since the relative lightness or heaviness of a boat has a lot to do with other characteristics to be discussed later on, I have set up the following table as a rough guide. The table gives the approximate weight in pounds for boats of moderate displacement at any given overall length.

A boat of 30 feet overall, for instance, that was significantly (say 30 percent) heavier than 8,000 pounds would be considered rather heavy displacement. Likewise, a 30-footer that weighed, say, 5,000 pounds would be quite light for its size.

The reason that the relative heaviness or lightness of a boat is important is that this factor determines certain fundamental characteristics of the behavior of the boat in the water.

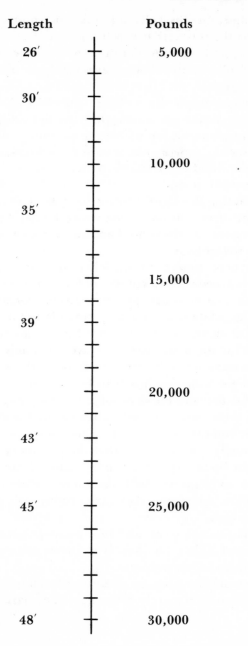

Length	Pounds
26′	5,000
30′	
	10,000
35′	
	15,000
39′	
	20,000
43′	
45′	25,000
48′	30,000

To illustrate this behavior, take an empty Band-Aid can and tape the top so that it will not leak. Get a block of wood about the same size and put the can and the block into a bathtub half full of water. Make waves with your hand and observe what happens.

The heavy-displacement boat — the block of wood — tends to be submerged by the waves while the light-displacement can bounces around on top of the waves, riding them and giving way to them. If these objects were indeed boats, which one do you think would be the drier? Which one would have the more comfortable motion?

Obviously, the light-displacement boat or Band-Aid tin, would be drier, but its motion would be more violent. Heavy-displacement, on the other hand, means an easier motion but a much wetter boat.

Right here, we are in the thick of the seaworthiness question which has been hotly contested for centuries. Many sailors maintain that heaviness per se means seaworthy. But we have seen that, while heaviness may mean less violent motion in a seaway, it also means taking lots of solid water on board. This means that the boat needs to be very strongly constructed in order to stand up to the repeated blows of the water.

The light boat, too, needs to be well built, because she has to be able to stand blows of solid water against her sides, even though these may be eased somewhat by the boat's ability to give way and thus absorb some of the blow.

All in all, it seems to me that the argument between heavy and light boils down to a tendency to equate heaviness with strength and lightness with flimsiness. While these equations may often be true, they are — today, at any rate — not necessarily so.

A boat can be weak and heavy just as surely as it can be strong and light. The key is *strength* rather than light or heavy, in and of themselves.

As you can see from the bathtub experiment, relative lightness or heaviness merely determines the characteristics of the motion of the boat in a seaway. Whether or not she will be able to endure in that seaway is determined finally by how well and truly she is made. This is why so much of Part 1 of this book is devoted to ways of enabling you to assess the fundamental structure of a boat.

2. Size

A boat is basically a box. This is to say that it has a length, a width and a height. Now, you know that if you increase one dimension of a box and increase the other two in proportion, the box gets a lot larger, very fast.

For an illustrative example, take four sugar cubes and arrange them into a larger cube, two units on each side. You have a box containing 4 cubic units and weighing 4 times whatever one of the basic cubes weighs.

Now increase each dimension of the box 50 percent, or by one cube. What is the size of the "box" now? Twenty-seven cubic units! So, by increasing each dimension of the box 50 percent, you have increased the size (and weight) of the box more than six times.

This same effect operates in the case of a boat and is the answer to the question, "If it's only 4 feet longer, why does it cost twice as much?"

A 30-foot boat is just about twice as much boat as a 26-footer having the same proportions: it weighs about twice as much and has twice as much interior, cubic space. This means twice the room for people, stoves, galleys, bunks, storage or whatever.

In other words, a lot more liveability with just a little more length.

Sheer size is important for many other reasons. One of the main ones is what is called stiffness, or the ability of the boat to stand up to its sail.

As you have seen, the hull of a boat can increase in three dimensions. The sail plan, on the other hand, can only increase in two dimensions.

Say you had a Boat A and scaled it up to Boat B by doubling all dimensions.

Boat B would be 8 times as heavy as boat A, but its sail area would be only 4 times as large.

Since it is the sail plan which tends to heel the boat and the weight of the hull is one of the factors that tend to counteract this heeling, the anti-heel forces gain faster than the heeling forces as the size of the boat increases.

3. Stability

In the discussion on size, we touched on one aspect of stability—the fact that the sail area (force that makes the boat heel) does not increase as fast as the hull weight or force that counteracts the sail plan.

There are several other factors in stability. Perhaps the most important of these is hull form.

Try this experiment: get an empty soft-drink can and seal up the opening with tape so water can't get in. Float it on its side in the sink or tub. Now get an empty cigar box or other flat-bottomed container, seal it and put it in the sink or tub, too.

Using a small bit of modeling clay, stand up a drinking straw on top of the cigar box. Try to do the same with the pop can.

Without going deeply into naval architecture theory, I think you can see that the cigar box has natural stability by virtue of its form (shape), and that the soft-drink can does not.

Now tape a lead weight under the can and try to set up the straw "mast" again. This will succeed, provided the lead weight is large enough—and you will obviously have a small model of a typical, ballasted sailboat.

The question logically arises: Why is it necessary to have the lead; why not just go with the flat-bottom, which has natural stability by virtue of its shape?

Of the several answers to this question, most important is probably that the cylinder, or the can, has less surface area in the water for a given weight—displacement—than the cigar box. Surface area in the water, the wetted surface, is a major deterrent to speed, and naval architects spend lots of time trying to reduce it as much as possible.

As a result, sailboat underbodies are a compromise between the cylinder and the cigar box. One of the ways you can judge the degree to which any boat relies on ballast or shape for stability is to walk around behind her and look at her underwater shape in cross section.

Photo A shows a boat which derives much of her stability from her shape—she is more like the cigar box than the soft-drink can. Photo B is the converse.

While you are studying the boat from this angle, keep in mind that the sail plan is the factor that works against stability. Thus, a shape like the cylinder, which derives all of its stability from the ballast, can be stiff—or sail at a small angle of heel—if the sail area is small. Yet, a shape like the

cigar box with ballast added—a very stable combination—can be tender, or sail at a large angle of heel, if the sail area is large and lofty.

Given the same sail plans, a boat that relies largely on ballast to keep her on her feet will need a relatively larger proportion of ballast than a boat whose hull has stability by virtue of its shape.

The proportion of ballast in a boat is found by dividing the weight of ballast by the weight, or displacement, of the boat. A boat displacing 15,000 pounds, having 7,500 pounds of ballast, has a ballast-to-displacement ratio of 50 percent.

Since we have seen that the underwater cross-sectional shape of the boat, as well as her rig, contribute importantly to her stability, it's pretty obvious that ballast ratio alone will not tell the story about the relative stiffness or tenderness of a boat.

4. Sail Area

The sail area of a boat is its power plant. And, since most

boats must sail in a wide range of wind strengths, it becomes an act of judgment to say just how much or how little sail a boat should have.

Here we are talking about her basic, working sails, since it is obviously possible to increase the area somewhat with such special sails as genoa jibs and spinnakers or to reduce the sail area by reefing.

What size basic rig a boat carries, therefore, depends upon the wind strength in which she is usually expected to operate.

Generally, a boat expected to sail in winds primarily in the range of 6 to 15 knots—summer conditions in the middle latitudes—will need basic working sail area (main and jib for a sloop) of about 100 square feet per ton (2,000 pounds) of displacement.

As mentioned before, however, small boats (below 30 feet) tend to have more than this and large boats (above 30 feet) tend to have less.

5. Speed

If the bathtub still has water in it from the earlier experiment, stick in a finger and wiggle it around to make some small waves. Notice the length of time it takes these waves to reach the far end of the tub.

Now put in your whole hand and make larger waves. You will notice that these waves move much faster through the water.

It is a basic fact of nature that a wave of a certain length moves through water at a given speed, and that the longer the wave, the higher the speed.

Scientists have clocked waves and found the formula which predicts the speed of any length wave. The formula is speed of wave in knots = 1.34 times the square root of the length of the wave in feet ($S = 1.34\sqrt{L}$).

Thus, a 25-foot long wave travels at 5 times 1.34 knots, or at 6.7 knots. A 900-foot long wave travels at 40.2 knots.

Now, a ballasted sailboat moving through the water makes

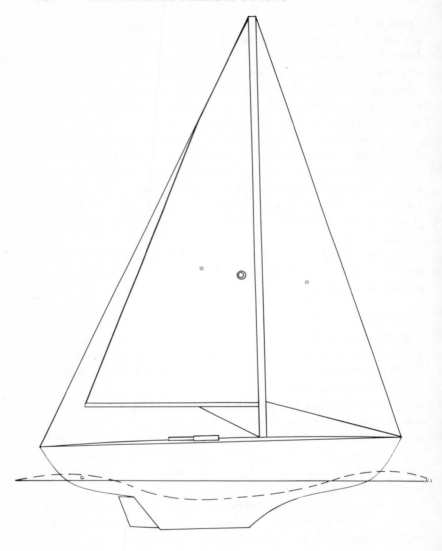

waves, and the faster she travels, the longer the waves she
makes. There comes a time when she is making one wave: one
crest of the wave is at the bow and the other is at the stern (see
sketch).

This is the largest wave she can make, and she can only travel as fast as this wave, which we know is limited by nature to $1.34\sqrt{L}$. As you can see from the sketch, the length of the wave made by the boat is going to fall somewhere between the overall length of the boat and its length at the waterline.

For practical purposes, therefore, you can estimate the speed potential of a ballasted sailboat by taking the square root of its waterline length and multiplying by 1.34. This speed is referred to as the hull speed of the boat.

To fully assess the speed potential of a boat, however, you need to know not only how *long* a wave she can be expected to make, by how *deep* a wave she can be expected to generate. Two waves can be the same length—travel at the same speed—but be of different depths.

Shallow waves are formed with less energy than deep ones and, since light boats make shallow waves, it can be seen that they need less power (sail area) to reach speed than do heavy ones.

This is to say that, for a given sail area and waterline length, a light boat will reach hull speed in lower wind velocities than will a heavy-displacement hull.

Part 3

Hulls and Rigs

Introduction

Basically, there are only two hull types in ballasted sailboats: the so called *full-run* keel with attached rudder and the *fin* keel with separated or spade rudder. There are many variations beween these types—fuller full keels and "finnier" fin keels.

What I have developed over the years is a mental spectrum into which I classify boats based on their hull type. I call it the "moose-to-butterfly" system. On the left end (moose), I put the really full-bodied, heavy-displacement type represented by Photo 23 On the right (butterfly), I place the really cutaway, light-displacement types represented by Photo 34 As you can see, many boats fall between .these two extremes; what I have done is to indicate under each picture the general behavior of each type.

23. (Moose) The underbody of this boat has a true full-run keel. Notice that the part of the bow of the boat that is underwater, the forefoot, is as deep as the rudder. Although only about 33-feet long, this boat probably weighs about ten tons. Her breeze is 20 knots, and, if there is much sea, she will be wet. In light air, she will be sluggish and the helm will feel "dead." Since she is mainly constructed of timber, there is very little interior room. The heart sure responds to this boat, though. She's truly traditional, right down to deadeyes and lanyards for the standing rigging.

24. Here is a small, (22-foot) moose of ferroconcrete. Note here that the forefoot is much more cutaway than the first boat. She also has relatively more beam. Her sailing characteristics will be similar to boat 23, but she will be easier to maneuver and turn because of the cutaway forefoot.

25-28. These boats represent relatively modern full-keel boats and are what most people think of when they say "traditional."

29. & 30. As you can see, the forefeet and bows are cut away to a much greater extent than are those in the truly traditional types pictured. The advantage of the bow and stern overhang is that they add to the reserve buoyancy of the boat and promote drier decks. The disadvantages of a lot of overhang is that it tends to promote pitching or "hobby-horsing" in a seaway. These boats are quite steady on the helm but need a fair amount of breeze to come alive. Years ago, I raced on a sister of boat 27, and I never really enjoyed her until one night, when we were going to windward with a deep-reefed main and small genoa in about 30 knots of breeze.

31. I put this type of boat in about the middle of the moose-butterfly spectrum. Although she is quite heavily cutaway underneath, her rudder is large and has a generous skeg in front of it. In light and moderate breezes, she is responsive; off the wind in a blow, she tracks extremely well because of the large skeg.

32. This is an early light-displacement production boat—26 feet long, she weighs less than 4,000 pounds. As you look at the rest of the pictures, you will see that her keel is relatively conservative when compared to the extreme butterfly boats pictured (Boats 33-34).

33. A highly successful racer of a few years ago. Practically unbeatable up-wind in 8 to 12 knots of breeze, she was trickier to steer off wind than boat 31 due to the absence of a skeg in front of the rudder. Boats 33 and 31 are the same overall length, but 31 weighs one ton more and is one foot wider.

34. This is currently (1976) about the limit in production fiberglass boats: it is a "butterfly." Note the extreme lack of underbody (and so, wetted surface) of boat 34. The keel is simply a blade formed by molding lead over a steel plate. It should be noted that butterflies are not necessarily small. There are 80-foot aluminum racers that are relatively lighter than boat 34.

1

Moose to Butterfly

As you can see, if sailing comfort is your object or if you are in an area where winds are usually strong, you would tend to pick a hull on the "moose" side of the spectrum. If the excitement of a livelier, more responsive boat is for you, or if you are in an area where winds are normally light to moderate, you might tend toward a "butterfly."

Bear in mind, too, as you look at these pictures, that I am assuming a normally proportioned rig on each of these hulls, around 100 square feet per ton (less for the heavy-displacement boats, more for the light).

I once owned a 31-footer much like the boat in Photo 38. She weighed 5500 pounds and had 500 square feet of sail (200 square feet per ton!), which is overrigging with a vengeance.

In 10 knots of breeze, she was a total delight. In 15 knots, she was on her ear and had to be reefed, even though she was 51 percent lead ballast.

I sold her a few years ago and on balmy summer afternoons,

I sometimes get wistful thinking about how she would tear up the water.

So far as general handling characteristics go, it can be said that the boats on the heavy side of the range are less sensitive to the helm and so tend to be easier to steer, requiring less concentration on the act of steering. They do, however, tend to build up large amounts of weather helm while reaching, due to the fact that the entire flow of water to windward (caused by the leeway of the boat) has to flow past the trailing edge of the rudder. With a separated rudder, the bulk of this water can flow between the keel and rudder.

Both types of hull can be made to sail themselves on the wind, since this is a function of the balance of the rig and the underbody, not of the basic shape. There are cranky boats of both shapes, of course. The fault is with the designer for not lining rig and hull up correctly; the fault is not in the basic shape of the hull.

The spade rudder boats do enjoy distinctly better handling characteristics under power; they are able to be turned in a tighter circle and to be steered in reverse. They also are much more sensitive to propeller torque and have distinct helm when under power; that is, if the helm is released, the boat will immediately round up.

This effect is considerably reduced by having a skeg in front of the rudder. A skeg also considerably improves downwind tracking under sail. All in all, I feel that an underbody like Photo 31 (Part 3, Chapter 1), if combined with a good, carefully balanced rig, represents the best of both worlds.

The most common rig on auxiliary sailboats is the sloop. The fundamental reason for this may be that it is less expensive to build a boat with one mast. But the fact remains that it is an excellent rig for general sailing and cruising.

I like the rig because it is simple to handle having, in normal circumstances, only two sails. With the powerful winches available today, handling large jibs is no particular problem.

Sailing a boat with two masts is often a bit like trying to sail two separate boats. It really is more work. Still, as with everything else, split rigs have their advantages, so let's discuss the two most commonly seen today—the yawl and the ketch.

The technical definition of a ketch is that it is two-masted, fore-and-aft rigged, with the after mast shorter than the forward, or main, mast. The aft mast is stepped *forward* of the rudder post.

The aft mast is called the mizzen, and it is important to note—if you want to be technically correct—that the mizzen is forward of the *rudder post,* not necessarily the helm or the position from which the boat is steered.

The ketch rig has many adherents. Its chief advantage is that many combinations of sail are possible. For instance, in strong winds a well-designed ketch can sail under her mizzen and working jib with main completely furled. Since many people find it easier to completely furl a main than to reef it, the ketch obviously has great appeal for them.

The chief disadvantage of the ketch is that, in a normal sailboat with aft cockpit, the mast is often in the way: it is right in front of the helm, as a rule, and also of the companionway. Careful design can pretty much eliminate this, but such design is the exception and not the rule.

From a distance, a yawl looks like a ketch with the exception that the mizzen on a yawl is relatively smaller than on a ketch and the mast is farther aft. The technical definition is this: in a yawl, the mizzen is *aft* of the rudder post.

Yawls became popular during the days of the CCA (Cruising Club of America) racing rule. Having a mizzen reduced the rating of a boat by quite a bit, and it was felt that the advantage of the lower rating more than made up for the additional windage and weight added by the mizzen. Basically, yawls are sloops with an afterthought. Perhaps they should be called hermaphrodite sloops!

In any case, there is an advantage to the yawl—and this goes for ketches, too. In strong seas where you have searoom, a yawl or ketch can often be hove-to by simply setting the mizzen alone and sheeting it in hard. The sail area aft tends to hold the boat close to the wind, and often the boat can be left to herself while the crew gets some rest. Also, at anchor, the mizzen can be used to keep the boat from swinging.

It is my feeling that, for general pleasure sailing and summer cruising in boats to about 35 feet, a sloop's the thing. Larger than this, a split rig starts to be appealing because, although it increases the number of sails that have to be handled, it decreases the size of those sails.

Further Reading

Sailing Yacht Design by Douglas Phillips-Birt. Tuckahoe, N.Y.: John de Graff, Inc., in association with Adlard Coles, Ltd.

Sailing Theory and Practice by C. A. Marchaj. New York: Dodd, Mead and Co., 450 pages.

Part 4

Used Boats

Introduction

The reasons for buying a used boat are primarily financial: used boats are less expensive than new boats. How much less usually depends upon the age of the used boat. It also depends upon the cost of a new boat offering the equivalent features of the used boat.

Thus, if a 1975 XYZ-35 costs $40,000 and $39,000 is being asked for a 1969 XYZ-35 with the same equipment, a used-boat buyer would be unlikely to buy the 1969 unless he knew that in 1969 the manufacturer had used platinum for ballast rather than lead.

Barring something of this sort, the informed potential buyer of the XYZ-35 is going to make the owner an offer lower than $39,000, an offer which to him represents the point at which he will decide to buy the boat new or look elsewhere.

Therefore, he might offer the owner, say, $32,500 — and the owner would probably agree to sell. In fact, he is very likely to sell because, in 1969, the present owner bought the boat new and complete for $28,500.

Yes, Virginia, the prices of new boats have gone up since 1969. As a matter of fact, between the fall of 1973 and the spring of 1974, the prices of new sailboats rose about 30 percent. As I pointed out in Part 1, most of the cost of a boat is the materials, so boat prices are naturally very sensitive to increases in the cost of materials.

If you are inclined to be put off and brood about these facts, pause and reflect upon what has happened to the market value of your house since you purchased it. Sailboats are very close to being real property, too. They are simple and are made of very durable materials.

A recent study of a Coast Guard cutter that had seen 20 years of hard service showed no weakening of the fiberglass sandwich of its hull. The Rhodes Bounty 40-footers that first were built almost 20 years ago are prized boats because they were extraordinarily strongly made due to initial conservatism in the use of a then-untried material, fiberglass.

I myself have been going happily to sea aboard a friend's 15-year-old retired ocean racer, a boat that won the Southern Ocean Racing Circuit (SORC) two years running and had really been pushed hard when my friend bought her.

So fiberglass sailboats are likely to be around for a long time. And, like houses, they are a reasonably good hedge against inflation. You might earn interest by keeping your dough in a savings bank, but you won't have nearly as much fun or adventure.

1

The Financial Side

If anything, used boats are a better investment than new ones. As I've said earlier, the material used for boats is very durable, and only the sails, engine and electronic instruments wear out at any appreciable rate.

Even then, engines can be replaced quite cheaply ($600 at this writing will rebuild and reinstall your present gasoline auxiliary engine). The same is true of sails and electronics. Except on out-and-out racing boats, these items are scarcely a significant part of the investment in an auxiliary sailboat.

Still, as the boat gets older, these things do wear out. Therefore, even though the capital part of a used boat becomes a higher percentage of the boat, the expenses are going to be higher, too. One kind of balances the other: less depreciation than with new, but higher expense.

As with new boats, financing is available for used boats on about the same terms. About 20 percent down payment will let you buy a used boat, assuming your credit history is good.

Generally, terms are limited to about seven years at a maximum, although there are signs this is changing.

Inflation and the rapidly rising prices of new boats are keeping the selling prices of used boats from going down; if anything, they are going up. This is particularly true of certain "key" used boats which have stood the test of time and which the market has found to be particularly desirable, for one reason or another. Some of these boats are discussed briefly in Chapter Four of this section of the book.

2

The 15-Minute Survey

A major difference between the purchase of a new boat and the purchase of a used boat is that the used boat carries no warranty. As a rule, this is explicitly stated on either the listing, which gives the written specifics of the boat, or the purchase agreement, which you sign when you make the initial commitment to buy.

Once the money has passed from you to the broker or owner and you have received the bill of sale, she's yours—virtue, vices, and all.

It is, therefore, even more important for you to satisfy yourself that the used boat is structurally sound. Now, normally, when you make an offer on a boat, your offer is contingent upon a marine survey carried out by a competent individual, most often a designer or naval architect whom you pay to go over the boat and to alert you, in a written report, of her defects.

Since this is a somewhat expensive procedure, about $5 per

foot overall length, it will help if you can at least make a reasonable appraisal of her yourself to determine whether the boat is sound enough for you to invest in a full-fledged survey.

The techniques for doing this are basically the same as those discussed in Part 1 of this book; namely, use your eyes and look at certain key areas of the boat.

As with a new boat, look at the lifelines and stanchions, seat lockers, hatches, hardware on deck. When you are below, open the easily accessible lockers and look at the hull-deck joint, both from the point of view of structure and to spot any signs of leakage.

If the lifeline stanchions (posts) show signs of leaking below, these can be sealed up. But leaking of the hull-deck joint can be a major problem that usually requires lifting the whole deck to properly fix.

A good area to look for leaking is in the hanging locker. No need to rip the boat apart; just look where you readily can. Inside the hanging locker is also a good place to check the secondary bonding of the bulkheads and chain plate attachments.

If the mast is stepped through the cabin, take a look at the mast step for signs of heavy corrosion. Check the bilge. This will reveal the general level of housekeeping the boat has had.

Be aware, though, that diesel-powered boats often have very black bilges due to the fact that these engines continually exude minute amounts of lubricating oil and diesel fuel from their many high-pressure fittings.

The stove condition and the head will also give a clue about prior care. Try the pressure pump on the stove and the pump in the head. The condition of all of these items will help you make an intelligent offer.

Just for a general impression, take a look at the engine. This won't tell you much except that it's there and whether it's a diesel or not (gas engines have spark plugs; diesels don't). Amazingly enough, owners sometimes don't know what kind of engine their boat has.

The exterior of the engine won't tell you much, in all probability, but you can ask some hard questions if it's badly rusted and shows signs of neglect—although I've seen some pretty vile-looking engines that ran beautifully and checked out fine on survey.

One that looks dead, however, might be dead! If there are sails below, pull the corner of one out of its bag to see if it seems reasonably clean and serviceable. Check for frayed edges and worn stitching.

All this doesn't take much time, but you will have given the once-over to the major aspects of the boat—deck, gear, hull-deck integrity, rig, engine, sails.

Don't, of course, take the time to do this unless the boat appeals to you for such other reasons as her looks, layout, finish or price. If the boat does appeal to you and you go through this process and find her worthy, you will be in a good position to make a realistic offer on the boat and to evaluate the survey report intelligently when you receive it.

Further Reading

Surveying Small Craft by Ian Nicholson. Camden, Maine: International Marine Publishing Co., 224 pages.

3

Buying a Used Boat Step by Step

There are two ways to buy a used boat: directly from the owner or through a broker. Since I am a broker, I propose to discuss the normal manner in which a used-boat sale takes place, since this is the way most used boats are sold.

The two principal functions of a broker are (1) to negotiate the terms of the sale, and see that they are carried out, and (2) to act as an escrow agent for the funds delivered by the buyer and for the bill of sale delivered by the seller until the terms of the sales agreement are complete. He then delivers the bill of sale to the buyer and the funds (less his commission) to the seller.

In carrying out these functions, the broker performs several other services. Chief of these is getting the information on the boat into the marketplace. This is done by means of a form called a listing (see illustration) that contains the written details of the boat's history, equipment and asking price.

These listings are usually kept in ring-binders arranged according to overall length of the boats. After your initial contact with a broker, he will usually suggest several possibilities to you and show you the written listings of boats he thinks would fit your requirements. Often this process covers several weeks: the broker calls you when he thinks he has something of interest for you or simply sends you a photocopy of the listing of the boat he feels should be of interest.

Brokers also advertise, and you should keep an eye on the ads. Sometimes an advertised boat will excite your interest and yet be in a location or of a type the broker does not have in mind for you. You can have him check it out for you.

Once you have found one or two boats that are particularly interesting, the next step is to go and see them. Be aware that finding a used boat involves a lot of running around. Just because a broker has a listing on a boat does not mean that she is just around the corner—our office has listings from as far away as Australia.

Let's say you have looked at several boats and zeroed in on one. You do the 15-minute survey and the boat looks good. What's next?

The next step is to make an offer through the broker. The normal procedure is for you to give the broker a deposit check for 10 percent of your offer and to sign a sales agreement which states the terms of your offer. Such a paper is filled out with the usual terms of a used boat or "brokerage" sale and is reproduced here.

This form is filled out as it might be in northern latitudes, where boats are laid up out of the water from fall until spring. Many sales take place during this period, when it is not possible to check the engine operation or condition of the electronics.

In order that the sale may go forward and title pass, the broker holds what is known as an "engine and electronics escrow." This is a sum of money withheld from the seller when the proceeds of the sale are paid over to him. If, when the boat is commissioned in the spring, something more than routine

PURCHASE AGREEMENT & DEPOSIT TICKET

I agree to purchase and hereby submit a deposit of $ *1950 —*

made payable to "ABC YACHT BROKERAGE"

for: *1974   XYZ 30*

as described in Listing # *72336*   (copy attached here)

Subject to: The seller's acceptance of my offer of $ *19,500 —*

             The seller's presentation of proper Bill of Sale

AND: *Survey*

       Financing

       $500 — engine and electronics

       escrow.

The seller certifies that the attached Listing # *72336*

is correct and that the above offer is acceptable.

It is understood that ABC YACHT BROKERAGE makes no representations
and takes no responsibility for the condition of the boat.

Seller	Buyer
E. D. Doakes	*J. D. Jones*

"ABC YACHT BROKERAGE"

BY: *H. W. Schlueth*   DATED: *9-5-75*

72336

ABC YACHT BROKERAGE

TYPE:	XYZ 30 AUX. SLOOP	ENGINE:	Universal Atomic 4, 30 HP gas built in 1974
LOA:	29'9 1/2"	TANKS:	Fuel - 20 gallons Water - 22 gallons
LWL:	25'		
BEAM:	9'6"	ELECTRICAL EQUIPMENT:	Two 12 volt batteries, control panel, battery selector switch, alternator
DRAFT:	5'		
HEADROOM:	6'1"	ELECTRONIC EQUIPMENT:	Fathometer, speedometer, log
BUILDER:	XYZ Yachts		
DESIGNER:	M. E. Wellknown		
YEAR:	1974		

CONSTRUCTION: Fiberglass hull and deck; blue haze hull, white deck; 3560# lead ballast; 8320# displacement

SAILS AND RIGGING: Main, jib, 150% genoa

Aluminum mast, stainless steel rigging, two rows jiffy reefing points, mainsail cover, genoa gear, mainsheet traveler, winch handles, Barient #22 genoa sheet winch, two halyard winches

ACCOMMODATIONS: She sleeps six (6) - "V" berths forward, convertible dinette, quarter berth with storage under

She has a marine head with sink

Galley equipped with sink, ice box, stove

GENERAL EQUIPMENT: Anchor, anchor line, chain, dock lines, fire extinguishers, life preservers, horn, fenders, boat hook, bilge blower, manual bilge pump, curtains, carpeting, fabric upholstery, bulkhead-mounted compass, bow and stern pulpits, single lifelines, boarding gate, screen, swim ladder, flag halyard

LOCATION: Westchester

PRICE: $21,000.00

The above information is believed to be correct, but it is not guaranteed. No representation about the boat's physical condition is made. Seller is to furnish proof of ownership at time of sale. 10% commission due when Sale is consummated.

commissioning of the engine or electronics is required—that is, if something is broken that could not have been discovered at the time of the survey—repair of the item is paid from the escrow funds.

Thus, the seller's liability is limited to the amount of the escrow. If the boat has an unusually large engine, or if the electronic gear should be unusually elaborate or complicated, the escrow will be larger.

This, too, is a negotiated item. You state what you want when you make your offer and, if the owner balks, you negotiate through the broker until an agreement is reached or not reached.

If there is no agreement because of price, because other terms of the offer are not met or because the boat fails survey after acceptance of the offer, then the broker returns your money.

If your offer is conditional on a satisfactory survey, say so in writing. Then, if the survey is not satisfactory, you can withdraw or change your offer. After you reach an agreement, which happens about 95 percent of the time, the broker will deposit your check and hold the funds until the survey is carried out.

Assuming the survey is satisfactory to you, and you or the broker has been able to arrange financing, the balance of the money is paid to the broker, who, by this time, has a signed bill of sale from the seller.

He gives the seller his net proceeds and you the bill of sale. And there you are, the proud possessor of a new light in your life.

I think it is a good time to say a few words about yacht brokerage. When you get to the point of deciding to buy a used boat, I think there are a few commonsense things you can do to ensure that you get a good view of the market and pay only the fair market price for the boat you decide on.

First off, I think you want to find a company that is

genuinely in the used boat business and that sells a sufficient number of boats of all sizes to have a good idea of what the market is, in fact, paying for X, Y or Z boat.

To do this, look at the ads in the brokerage section of a national magazine such as *Yachting* or *Sail* or *Motor Boating* to see which companies put forth a respectable list of boats of the size and type you are interested in.

Many companies sell both new and used boats, and a close look at their ads will show you where the emphasis is. Nationally available, in a library if not at a local newsstand, you can look at the boating advertisements in the sports section of the *New York Times* every Sunday with the same thoughts in mind: who seems to be in the used boat business and who doesn't?

Further along these lines, you may want to try to assess the broker with whom you are dealing. There is no graduate degree in yacht brokerage, you know; so you won't see a degree on the wall to attest to his competence. Most states do not require that yacht brokers be licensed. Yacht brokers are self-taught, and their degrees of knowledge and experience can differ vastly. As you talk with different brokers, try to decide what kind of job he can do for you. Evaluate him the same way you would evaluate a doctor, dentist, lawyer, teacher—unless you assume competence with those people just because they have embossed paper hanging on the walls.

Remember that, although the seller is paying this individual from the proceeds of the sale, you are in a sense able to hire his brain to ferret out the right boat for you from among a wealth of possibilities. This means that you are relying on his experience and integrity to see you safely—and sanely—through the entire process of buying a used boat. Choose your broker carefully!

4

"Key" Used Boats

As you undoubtedly realize by now, there is no perfect boat, just as there is no perfect anything else. Like people, boats have warts and have to be accepted (or rejected) as a whole. It is easy to fault individual items on practically any boat, but what you are buying, finally, is a whole complex of many factors. So you have to come to the conclusion when you select your boat that, on balance, she suits your intended purpose.

The list that follows is made up of brief descriptions of boats that, to my mind, have, in the main, successfully resolved the many elements that go together to make up a total boat. By and large, these boats have passed the tests of time and the market. Their qualities, good and bad, are well-known, and it is my feeling that, if you are seriously considering a boat in any particular size range, you would be wise to take a look at the boats on this list in the same general size or price range, because the boats here continue to be sought after in the marketplace. They are not will-o'-the-wisps.

In using this list, please remember that the prices given are approximate and based on sales taking place in the fall of 1976.

Bristol 22' Caravelle ($5,000-$6,000)

The proportions of this boat are exceptional. She is a handsome little vessel with exceptional room below and a proper-sized cockpit for a cruiser. She sails fast and dry for her size. She comes as near anything I've seen to what used to be called a "tabloid cruiser."

Columbia 22' ($5,000-$6,000)

Her proportions are not quite as pleasant as the Bristol's, but her design emphasis is a little different: relatively more space is allotted to the cockpit, and so she is more day sailer/cruiser than an out-and-out cruiser. A realistic choice for the way most people actually use boats in this size range.

Pearson 22' ($5,000-$6,000)

Designed as a MORC (Midget Ocean Racing Club) boat, she is low and light and much less roomy than the Bristol or Columbia. Still, she is very easy to look at and, like many successful racing boats, a real witch under sail.

Sailstar Corsair 25' ($6,000-$7,000)

A very unusual boat. She has nearly 6' of headroom and yet the overall look of the boat is traditionally pleasing. Her roominess is achieved by a quite deep and full underwater hull shape, but the price paid is tenderness. She heels to a rather large angle quickly before stiffening up — remember the soft-drink can.

Islander Excalibur 26' ($6,500-$7,500)

Very light, very fast, great fun to sail. The house is low and so is the headroom below — 4'11". But you have excellent visibility from the cockpit. Generally, sailing qualities are weighted more heavily in this design than creature comforts. In our area, she was top MORC boat for several years until the advent of the Ranger 26.

Pearson 26' ($8,500-$11,000)

Introduced at the New York Boat Show in 1970, this boat to date has reached hull number 1,300. The chief reasons for this astounding success are the fact that most women can stand up in it (headroom 5'8"), it has a sensible layout which includes a private head; and it marked a turn on the part of the manufacturer to a less expensive type of interior, thereby saving money and resulting in a price advantage, in 1970, of a solid $1,000.

Pearson Ariel 26' ($6,500-$7,500)

Headroom is achieved in this boat by raising the after portion of the cabin above the forward part into what is called a dog house. As a result, the hull form is a stiffer one than the Corsair's. Like the Corsair, she has a full-run keel of the modern type. Some have inboard engines, and these generally sell for $500 to $1,000 more than the outboard-powered models. She will outsail the Corsair, but not the Excalibur.

Ranger 26' ($9,000-$11,000)

Like the Excalibur, this boat is somewhat shy of headroom (5'5") and, as in the Excalibur, the view from the cockpit is excellent for this reason. The boat has had quite a successful racing career in our area and, while not at the top anymore, she is a good all-around boat that has the advantage of being very good looking.

C & C 27' ($16,500-$18,500)

A totally modern fin-keel, spade-rudder boat which somehow gets 6'1" of headroom into this size while keeping visibility from the cockpit, stiffness, speed and striking beauty of line. Only introduced in 1971, more than 500 C & C 27s are now sailing.

Tartan 27' ($13,000-$16,500)

At the other end of the spectrum from the C & C, this little keel-centerboarder has a full-run keel with attached rudder. Her shallow draft makes her desirable in bay areas. Begun in the early 1960s, this boat continues to sell steadily, year after year. Our office recently had the happy chance to sell boat Number 600. Despite my general attitude toward split rigs, I find this boat is particularly appealing as a yawl.

Pearson Triton 28' ($9,500-$13,000)

Production began in 1959 on this very conservative design. She has a full-run keel with attached rudder and offers 6' of headroom, enclosed head and inboard power. When production ceased in 1967, more than 750 Tritons had been sold. The boat is narrow by today's standards, but an awful lot of people have sailed many miles in Tritons. I doubt there will ever cease to be a market for Tritons.

Allied Seawind 30' ($16,000-$22,000)

The first fiberglass boat to sail around the world, this boat is usually rigged as a ketch. Her hull form is conservative, short-ended and full. As a result, she is initially somewhat tender, but this probably promotes an easy motion at sea, and the boat is an excellent all-around boat even if she's on the slow side.

Dufour Arpege 30' ($16,000-$25,000)

A strikingly original boat at the time of her introduction (about 1967) and still so. By placing the head all the way forward in the bow of the boat, the designer was able to create an interior layout that includes a large, sit-down chart table and berths located so that all are usable when the boat is underway. If you plan to do much sailing at night, look at this boat.

Pearson 30' ($18,000-$20,000)

Like the C & C 27, a fin-keel, spade-rudder boat and an even bigger market success. Introduced in 1971, there are now nearly 900 Pearson 30 owners. With this boat, the manufacturer capitalized on the lessons learned from their 26: people did not necessarily judge a boat solely by its interior. You could go to a plainer interior provided you did not strip the essential boat and did pass the savings along. The boat is big, strong, good looking, well-mannered, fast and has a thoroughly sensible layout.

Bristol 32' ($19,000-$22,000)

This boat, like the two that follow, has the modern full-keel, attached-rudder underbody and, while on the slow side, she's a handsome, traditional-looking craft, well-suited to leisurely cruising.

Pearson Vanguard 32' ($17,000-$18,500)

When first introduced in 1964, a Vanguard equipped to race cost about $21,000; cruise-equipped, about $18,000. A good illustration of the fact that money invested in a fiberglass sailboat is just that—an investment, not an expense.

Allied Luders 33' ($24,000-$26,500)

This boat has a fuller underbody than either the Vanguard or Bristol 32 and is highly prized among cruising sailors. She has a reputation for being very strongly made—a point upon which you can satisfy yourself using the techniques of Part 1 of this book.

Morgan 34' ($19,000-$23,000)

Designed by an avid sailer, this boat has wide decks, low house for good visibility from the cockpit and very good looks. She is the shoalest of the keel centerboarders, drawing only 3'3" with the board housed. The normal underbody is full run with attached rudder, although a few were made in 1968 with spade rudders separated from the keel. Introduced in 1967, the earlier boats are prized because they have bronze centerboards. Two layouts were made and both are popular, although I personally prefer the aft galley model.

Tartan 34' ($22,000-$26,000)

Like the Luders, Tartans have a reputation for great strength. This boat has been in production for about 10 years. The underbody is the more modern fin with a large skeg in front of the rudder. The Tartan is a keel-centerboarder and, due to her shoal draft, is highly prized by shoal-water sailors and gunkholers.

Allied Seabreeze 35' ($27,500-$33,500)

Very similar to the Pearson in looks, the interior is richer: Allied continued with teak bulkheads when Pearson switched to Formica after 1968. Also a keel-centerboarder with full-run underbody.

C & C 35' ($28,500-$33,500)

This was a true breakthrough boat that demonstrated that it was possible to have a fast, highly competitive boat that was a superb cruiser due to strength and good, sensible layout. To top it all, she's beautiful—not in a traditional way, but in a modern way all her own.

Hinckley Pilot 35' (33,500-$60,000)

A very traditional design with low topsides and sweeping sheer line. While somewhat narrow and cramped by today's standards for a 35-footer, this boat, like all Hinckleys, is very strongly made, beautifully and lavishly finished with varnished natural woods.

Pearson 35' ($28,500-$33,500)

One of the few traditional-looking, full-keel boats remaining in production, she has reasonably shoal draft, thanks to a centerboard. Her distinctive characteristics are: largest cockpit of any boat her size, greatest headroom (6'4" throughout) and a truly private forward cabin.

Pearson Alberg 35' (21,000-$25,000)

Big brother to the Ariel and Triton, very much like the Luders in hull form, this is the boat that introduced hot and cold pressure water and showers to small cruising boats. Like the Luders, although no longer built, they are much sought after by conservative sailors.

Chris Craft Apache 37' ($21,000-$24,000)

This is an early fin-keel, spade-rudder design. The keel is made of cast iron and is bolted into the canoe body of the boat. The boat is very good looking and has a reputation for strength. Close-reaching in fresh breezes, a well-sailed Apache can stay with many of the more modern designs.

Islander 37' ($25,000-$28,500)

Great room below and an appealing interior finish have kept this boat popular. Although she doesn't rate well under the current racing rule, she is quite fast in an absolute sense, due to her modern underbody. In appearance she is a nice blend of traditional and modern elements.

Pearson 39' (about $45,000)

This is a modern keel-centerboarder with a separated rudder mounted on a large skeg. Like the Pearson 35, she has a nice private cabin forward and her layout includes a sit-down chart table aft, opposite the galley. Also like the 35, she has an unusually large cockpit which promotes comfort under sail and later, at anchor, when the cocktail flag is hoisted.

Cal 40' (about $30,000)

This is the boat that really blasted a hole in the theory that a light boat could not be strong and seaworthy. In the ten years following her introduction, she dominated racing; as a result, the Cal 40 is thoroughly tested in the school of hard knocks—ocean racing. The boat weighs only 15,000 pounds and has a fin keel (which is conservatively very long, by today's standards) and a free-standing spade rudder. With the racing rule change from CCA to IOR, so many Cal 40s came on the market that three years ago you could buy a used one for about $20,000. But no more.

Hinckley Bermuda 40' ($60,000-$95,000)

This boat has been in production so long that it is hard to indicate a price: $60,000 is about what boats built in the early '70s have been bringing. Earlier vintages may bring less, but it is difficult to imagine even the oldest selling for less than $40,000 if it's at all well-kept; new Bermuda 40s are over $100,000. These boats are superbly built and finished and have been thoroughly wrung out by hard racing and long-distance voyaging. The hull configuration is traditional, with sweeping sheer and low cabin trunk. She is a keel-centerboarder with attached, barn-door rudder.

Rhodes Bounty 41' ($21,000-$26,000)

One of the very earliest boats to be built in fiberglass in the U. S. and, as a result, they tend to be very much overbuilt. For this reason, they are sought by super-conservative sailors and those with serious intentions of cruising oceans. By today's standards, they are too narrow to allow spacious accommodations, and the cockpits are small. But these are actual virtues in the eyes of an incipient ocean voyager.

Rhodes Reliant 41' ($39,500-$43,000)

With this boat, Phil Rhodes took a layout that had previously been used only in much larger boats and adapted it to a 40-footer. This layout has an aft cabin and aft cockpit and is exceedingly flexible. In normal cruising, it means there are two private cabins in the boat, one forward and one aft. At sea, there is a private cabin aft, but not so far aft that the bunks are unusable in rough going. In appearance she is quite traditional and the underbody is full run with attached rudder.

5

Case History

In the fall of 1969, Mr. and Mrs. Jones came into our office looking, they said, for a fairly recent, used 26-footer. After talking with them for a while, I learned they had a 22-footer with which they had been sailing and cruising for two years. One of the things they wanted to know was whether they could trade in their present boat.

I said our company would take their present boat if they bought a new boat. Since a used boat, however, ordinarily belonged to an individual and not to our company, it was not normally possible to arrange a swap. I suggested that they had a choice to make: to own no boat for a while or to own two boats for a while.

That is, they had either to sell their boat and then look for a replacement or buy their next boat and then sell their present boat.

Well, they decided they would go with the second choice. That way, they would not run the risk of being boatless if they were unable to find a suitable 26-footer by spring.

Having by now spent some time talking with the Joneses about their boat, and what they liked and did not like about it and other boats, I had in mind a boat I thought would suit them right down to the ground. It was the used 26 I had shown to the Smiths earlier.

Mrs. Jones liked the boat very much and, unlike Mrs. Smith, was not the least put off by the rusty can rings in the icebox. A little Zud, she said, would take them off right away. Mr. Jones liked the boat, too, and wanted to know what was being asked.

When I told him, he was surprised. He had been watching the *New York Times* ads, and the price I had given him was about $1,000 below the normal asking price of $8,000.

I told him that the boats were actually trading hands for about $7,500, and that it looked to me like this owner really wanted to sell the boat and was simply being realistic.

Mr. Jones seemed to think there might be something wrong with the boat, so I suggested that he and I look at the boat closely together and essentially do a fifteen-minute survey.

We did this and the boat looked good to both of us. I then suggested that he buy the boat, since the price asked was more than fair—or that he at least make the owner a slightly lower offer.

At this point, Mr. and Mrs. Jones demurred. It was the first boat they had seen and they just couldn't decide that fast. I replied (sounding very much like a high-pressure salesman, I'm sure) that that was because I had gone through a process of selection for them and felt this boat most nearly fit their requirements.

Well, they were still hesitant, so in order to clear the air and let them relax, I suggested that we look at two or three other boats in the same size and price range. We climbed down the ladder, and, as we were walking toward my car, one of the other brokers at our office came by with a nicely dressed young couple and asked for the key to the 26.

You guessed it. In the time it took us to drive around to the other boats, the young couple made an offer $250 lower than the price asked, and the owner agreed to sell. I wasn't too surprised, because this kind of thing happens daily in our business. But the Joneses were flabbergasted. They had no idea things could happen so fast. Boats, after all, are luxuries not to be snapped up like necessities.

Boats may be luxuries, but after eight years of selling them, I can tell you they carry a heavy emotional freight. Perhaps this is because of the Walter Mitty in all of us, perhaps to other things, but a clean boat fairly priced does not sit around lonely for long. And this is as true in a recession as in a boom. Maybe it's truer in a recession because, while people watch their pennies, they don't stop buying boats.

I eventually found the Joneses another boat of the same type and they bought it for the fair market price. Their indecision cost them about $750, but I don't think they acted wrongly. They didn't know me well enough to evaluate my baloney quotient, if you will, and were simply being conservative by wanting to test the market further before making a decision.

It was frustrating for me because I knew to a certainty that that 26 was the right boat for the Joneses and, in fact, they reached the same conclusion. It was also frustrating for them, as any lost opportunity is.

The main point of this story is, I guess, that sailboats are considered a good thing in this country, and good things have a ready market in the United States.

6

Steel Sailboats

Several years ago, while I was seriously contemplating going to sea with my family, my search for strength in a boat led me to steel. My conclusion today is that, all in all, steel is a fine material for a sailboat. Aluminum may be stronger, pound for pound, but it also is more susceptible to electrolytic corrosion and requires a more sophisticated welding technique that depends upon an inert gas to shield the area being welded to prevent the weld from oxidizing.

Steel, on the other hand, is not as active electrically and the welding technique does not require the same level of sophistication in either equipment or operator skill. Indeed, with only 30 hours of welding experience under my belt, I am satisfied that I could satisfactorily patch a steel boat. It might not be the best-looking weld in existence, but it would be strong and serve until a real pro could get at it.

The great French circumnavigator, Bernard Moitessier, relates in one of his books that he was able to patch a hole in his boat with a hand drill and bolts and that the patch held for many, many tough miles at sea.

The bugaboo about steel in the minds of most people is, of course, rust. Well, over the course of nearly eight years as a yacht broker, I've been involved in the sale of several steel boats, and I am satisfied that this is not as severe a problem as you might think.

Most recently I was the broker in the sale of a 12-year-old, 41-foot steel sloop that had not been painted in about four years. Upon survey, the inside of the hull turned out to be very nearly corrosion free. At the time this vessel was built, the inside of the hull had been sprayed with epoxy resin that had apparently fused itself to the steel as a thoroughly satisfactory protective skin.

The outside of the hull, however, did reveal a problem caused by an innate factor of the fabrication process: due to the great heat generated in welding, it is virtually impossible to have a perfectly fair steel hull. As the welds cool, there is a tendency for slight hollows and ripples to develop. Because this boat was a yacht, it was felt necessary to fill these hollows with a glazing compound and trowel it to produce a fair smooth surface that was then sanded carefully and painted. What happened was that water vapor penetrated this fairing compound, lifted it and began corroding the steel. Eric Hiscock mentions this same problem in his recent book, *Sou'west in Wanderer IV*.

The solution is obvious: sandblast the hull down to bright metal, paint it and accept a few bumps and hollows as part of the price paid for the great strength of steel. One of the large oil companies—Mobil, I believe—has developed a paint for their tankers, which would seem to me to be an excellent choice for a steel yacht. Done this way, the hull could probably go four or five years before repainting, assuming care was taken not to score or scratch the paint.

Another problem with steel hulls has been with the anti-fouling paint on the bottom. In the past, virtually all effective bottom paints contained large amounts of copper. Immersed in salt water, copper and steel make a battery and the steel gets eaten away. To prevent this, the steel had to be separated from the copper by carefully applied layers of inert paint that formed a barrier between the copper and steel. Woolsey Paint Company, however, has now come out with an anti-fouling paint for steel boats that uses something other than copper as the poison.

All in all, my investigation of this material has led me to believe that it is probably more expensive to maintain than fiberglass — but quite a bit less expensive than wood. And, with steel you can get not only a strong hull, but also a very nearly watertight one. All seams are welded and the hull, deck and cabin are truly fused into one unit.

To mount things like lifeline stanchions on a steel boat, you don't drill holes that will sooner or later leak; you weld them to the deck or bulwarks. This, briefly, is why steel seems to be a preferred material for the really serious voyagers like Hiscock and Moitessier.

Further Reading

Must reading if you want to consider a steel sailboat is *Boatbuilding with Steel* by Gilbert C. Klingel. Camden, Maine: International Marine Publishing Co., 248 pages.

7

Wood Sailboats

There is very little on earth as appealing as a wood sailboat, especially one of traditional character designed by a master like Olin Stephens, John Alden or Aage Nielsen and built by such a master builder as Henry Nevins. I still think the most beautiful boat I ever saw was "Bolero," designed by Stephens and built by Nevins. A close second is the schooner "Brilliant," designed and built by the same pair. The last boat I owned was a Nevins-built design by Stephens. She was 31 feet long, 6 feet wide, 37 years old — and an absolute witch under sail.

The emotional appeal of wood being what it is, I have watched innocent people over the years become embroiled in affairs with some of these sirens. Mostly, things turn out all right and the people involved emerge a little poorer, somewhat saddened and thoroughly inoculated against another bout of wood-boat fever. They go on to a stock fiberglass boat and are where they should have been in the first place.

Sadly, the wood boat is often not so fortunate. It is possible to really damage a wood boat through simple innocent ignorance. To take just one factor as an example, good ventilation is very important to the health of a steel boat — but it is absolutely critical to a wood boat. You can leave a glass boat shut up tight and untended for months while, say, you take a vacation in Europe. You will probably come back to find the inside of the boat black with mildew, but structurally it will be unaffected. Do this to a wood boat and you may very well destroy her. What is mildew in a glass boat becomes rot in a wood boat.

Briefly, it takes a lot of knowledge to own a wood sailboat. This is true because a wood boat is an intricate mesh of many different kinds of woods fitted together in a very specific pattern, much like a Chinese puzzle. Like the puzzle, each piece depends upon the other. Weaken one and the whole structure weakens.

I have not written this so much to discourage anyone from owning a wood boat, but rather as one friend might counsel another on the brink of marriage. There are simply many more factors involved in owning wood than there are in any other material. I am going to go into some of these next, but right now I would advise anyone who feels the appeal of wood to become pretty conversant with the two books listed at the end of this chapter.

To begin with, there is the factor of the wood itself, specifically with its seasoning. To be really suitable for use in a boat, wood needs to be allowed to season, or rest, after being cut into timbers and planks until its water content is about 15 percent.

This used to be acomplished by builders such as Nevins by carefully stacking wood in roofed but sideless sheds. This way, the wood was open to the free play of air yet protected from rain and snow. The rule of thumb was that boat-building wood should be allowed to season one year per inch of thickness. You can easily see what this meant in terms of time and capital tied up.

The reason for this great care is that the seasoning is a large factor in the prevention of rot after the boat is built. In order to grow, the fungus that rots wood needs a warm, stagnant, moist environment and wood with a moisture content of about 25 percent. So the name of the game in wood boat-building was to start with the wood at a much lower moisture content and then construct the boat in a way that would first keep water away from the wood or allow it to run off if it did penetrate into the interior of the boat.

Specifically, the great danger is the build-up of fresh water or high humidity inside the boat. Salt water is inimical to the growth of the fungus and you will rarely find rot in the under-body of a boat used in salt water. Preventing the buildup of humidity is why ventilation is so critical to a wood boat.

From the above considerations come most of the additional costs of owning a wood boat. Maintenance of the protective barriers against fresh water require that virtually everything on the exterior of the boat be painted or varnished every year. Since the most important aspect of painting is care in preparation of the surface, this obviously takes time and a degree of skill. Labor rates in our area are $20 per hour, so where a figure of $60 per foot per year will maintain a glass boat, you should figure about double that for a wood boat. That is, unless you have the skills and don't count the cost of your own time working on the boat.

Now, there are other ways to construct a boat out of wood, and one of the best is called "cold molding." In this process, thin strips of wood are laid over a mold of the boat, criss-cross on top of each other, and are glued or held together with epoxy resin. In this manner, the wood is sealed from the penetration of water vapor and rot does not occur. Any desired thickness can be achieved and structurally it is ex-cellent for a boat—strong, rigid and very light.

The interior and exterior of the boat are often left finished "bright," or as though varnished with the beautiful grain and colors of the wood showing as in fine furniture. Many racing boats are being built this way today, which means that we cruising types can look forward to some practical wood boats on the used market in the years to come.

Further Reading

Boatbuilding by Howard I. Chapelle. New York: W. W. Norton and Co., 624 pages.

Yacht Designing and Planning by Howard I. Chapelle. New York: W. W. Norton and Co., 373 pages.

8

The Formal Survey

Having done a fifteen-minute survey and reached agreement on price with the seller of the boat, the next step is
to have her formally surveyed by an individual who is competent to do this work. Usually this is a naval architect,
although other individuals, such as brokers of long experience,
could also do this work.

Obviously, the broker who is handling your negotiation can't
do the survey. He can, however, give you several names of
people in the area who do surveys, and you can contact them
and qualify them as best you can. You are doing the hiring,
and the surveyor works for you for a fee that is based on the
size of the boat.

How to pick a good surveyor? Here are some suggestions: if
the company through which you are buying the used boat is
also in the new boat business, ask who surveys their trades. Ask
a broker at a company other than the one through which you
are buying the boat. Ask around at your club or among any

friends you may have who sail and who have bought and sold several boats.

Okay, then, you've hired the surveyor. What should you expect? Basically, a very thorough and more extensive examination of the areas into which you looked during your fifteen-minute examination of the boat. Having done the fifteen-minute survey yourself, you should have a good idea of what to expect; you will have taken this into account in the price you offered. What you want from the surveyor is an indication of anything surprising.

Normally, the surveyor will not go to the extreme lengths discussed in Ian Nicholson's book, *Surveying Small Craft*, but he will take a slow look at everything he can see (survey on 30 to 40-foot boats takes about 4 hours) and give you a written report of his findings. He will, for example, go over the surface of the hull with a wood hammer, tapping lightly to find any "voids," or areas in which the glass roving was not saturated with resin and which, therefore, are structurally weak.

To better fix this in your mind, I have selected three surveys that appear on the following pages. Survey One is a bad survey, and, obviously, the boat is virtually destroyed and nearly worthless.

Survey Two is a mildly alarming survey, but, upon examination, it consists of a collection of items that are fairly readily fixable. The surveyor's opinion is that these items are beyond what the buyer of a used boat of that size and price has a right to expect, especially considering the young age of the boat. The price of this boat was negotiated downwards, buyer and seller agreeing to split the costs of the repairs. An eminently reasonable solution, since the buyer was going to enjoy the major benefit of those repairs.

Survey Three reflects an unusually well-loved boat, and the surveyor feels that the items noted are normal and to be considered part of the routine maintenance of the boat. He also feels that no concessions on price should be expected from the seller.

Survey One

June 19, 1975   File No. 321

Mr. E. C. James
White Oak Point
Mt. Holly, VA

Dear Mr. James:

This report constitutes the findings of the undersigned, for a
survey performed June 18, 1975, on the XYZ 28, Chaos, located
at City Island, New York.

Year Built - 1969

Hull Serial Number - 123

Engine Serial Number - 72336

General

This particular yacht has been neglected and abused in just about
every respect. There has been little, if any, preventive maintenance performed, and it certainly shows. Quite frankly, unless
steps are taken immediately to rectify some of the major items,
I consider this boat to be a floating accident waiting to happen.
I would not, under any circumstance, recommend that you purchase
this boat in its present condition.

The following deficiencies were noted:

1. The boat is extremely filthy with large amounts of mildew
in all of the lockers, plus about one inch of slime in the
bilge.

2. The fiberglass taping of the molded interior components to
the inside of the shell has delaminated to a great extent in
the following areas. This delamination is allowing the shell
to flex unduly in each area.

    a. Forepeak bulkhead to shell

    b. Aft end of the forward vee-berth to shell

    c. Inboard side of hanging locker to shell

    d. Toilet room sink counter to shell

    e. Inboard side of galley sink counter to shell

    f. Fore and aft dinette seats to shell

    g. Inboard side of starboard quarter berth to shell

2. Cont'd.

The delamination of the glass taping at the above joints will continue unless the entire affected areas are removed and re-glassed by competent workmen.

3. The majority of the wiring system is poorly done with many loose, unconnected wires, taped connections and terminals lo-cated where water leakage can easily short the whole system out.

4. The covers on the forward vee-berth cushions have large tears in them and these covers should be replaced.

5. The mooring cleats on the foredeck show signs of leakage around the fasteners. These fittings should be removed, re-bedded and refastened.

6. The fiddles on the forward cabin shelves, port and starboard, are loose and require refastening.

7. The plywood inspection plate in the forward vee-berth is loose and requires refastening.

8. The upper shroud chainplate lug through bolts are loose and should be tightened.

9. The hull to deck joint is in poor shape with visible signs of it leaking in numerous places. At the joint of the transom and deck, port side, it is possible to stick a probe right through to the inside of the boat.

10. The installation of the gasoline tank must violate every safety standard known to mankind. The tank is just lying on top of the starboard quarter berth with no hold down straps or chocks whatsoever. It is very possible that this tank will break loose from the fill pipe and slide into the main cabin.

11. The engine access hatch is loose and adrift and the cockpit can not be considered watertight. This hatch should be bedded down and securely fastened to the cockpit sole.

12. The lower eye swage fittings on the port aft lower shroud, port upper shroud, port forward lower shroud and starboard forward lower shroud have hairline cracks on their upper ends, caused apparently by stress corrosion. The above shrouds would have to be replaced.

13. The weld connecting the starboard spreader to the mast is badly cracked and unless rectified immediately, there is a good chance that the rig will be lost in the very near future.

14. A much heavier jib tack snap shackle is required over the existing fitting.

15. The starboard forward and aft bases of the bow pulpit are loose and probably leaking. These fittings should be removed, rebedded and refastened.

16. The entire gel coated exterior surfaces of this boat are in poor condition. There are a great many places where digs, gouges, and scratches have been filled, but not sanded, and other areas where no attempt has been made to cover them. If any consideration was made to restore this boat to even good condition, the entire deck and hull topsides would have to be painted.

It is the intent and spirit of this report to provide a true and unbiased opinion of the defects of the vessel and to its equipment, elaborating on the defects and the equipment that are in need of replacement or repair. Latent defects and damages not to be found without opening up or removing ceiling, joiner work, deck coverings, fittings, or tanks, etc., and/or disassembling machinery, plumbing, concealed wiring or other parts of this vessel, are not intended to be covered by this survey. The undersigned shall suffer no liability for not being able to properly evaluate parts, machinery, and equipment of the hull as stated above. Acceptance of this report shall constitute agreement of the foregoing.

Respectfully submitted,

John Doe

John Doe
Naval Architect
Marine Surveyor

Survey Two

March 29, 1976

Mr. Charles Jones
92 Hickory Drive   File No. 1234
Larchmont, New York

Dear Mr. Jones:

This report constitutes the findings of the undersigned for a
pre-purchase survey performed on your behalf on the ABC 36,
ILOILO. The boat was surveyed on March 27, 1976, while hauled
out and in winter storage at the XYZ Yacht Yard.

Year Built - 1973

Builder - ABC Yachts

Hull Registration No. - ABC07023373

Hull No. - 23

Engine Serial No. - 72336

Type Engine - Westerbeke 4-60 diesel

General

This boat has seen a great deal of use and abuse for her age, and
it is a tribute to her builder and not her owner that she still
is in presentable condition.

The overall structural integrity of the fiberglass hull and deck
appears to be sound. No structurally deficient voids in the hull
to deck joint, bulkhead to shell joint, or molded interior to
shell joints were discovered.

Deficiencies

1. The propeller shaft "cutless" bearing housed in the strut is
completely worn out and must be replaced.

2. Both propeller blades are heavily nicked from contact with
flotsam. The propeller requires either reconditioning or replacing.

3. The trailing edge of the ballast keel, starboard side, requires
filling with epoxy putty. (Marked with yellow crayon).

4. There are four (4) quite small, non-structural voids in the gel coat of the sellel's underbody (three (3) starboard, one (1) port, approximately amidships, marked with yellow crayon). These voids should be rough sanded and filled with an epoxy putty.

5. This vessel has gone hard aground at one time. As a result, there are six (6) small, deep gouges in the forebody, just below the waterline caused by hitting a sharp object. The impact has also caused a crazing of the port topside gel coat in way of the forepeak bulkhead and the attachment of the forward cabin veeberth. No other damage was discovered.

There is little that can be done about the gel coat crazing, but the gouges in the underbody should be filled with a good epoxy putty even though the hull laminate is sound and quite thick in this particular area.

6. The gel coated topsides of this boat are in <u>terrible</u> condition and reflect both hard use and poor seamanship. There is not much that can be done to the many scratches and nicks present, except to give the topsides a good compounding and waxing. If a true yacht finish is desired, the only recourse would be to paint the topsides.

7. Every chain plate shows signs of leakage where the lug protrudes through the deck. The finishing plates should be removed and the watertight bedding compound seal around each lug should be removed.

8. The toilet discharge sea cock under the port settee is very difficult to operate, and requires a good lubrication.

9. The flexible rubber portion of the stove fuel-feed line should be replaced. The present hose is of insufficient length to allow the stove to swing freely in its gimbals.

10. The engine heat exchanger, remotely located in the starboard cockpit-locker, is loose from its mounted position. The plywood board that the exchanger is bolted to should be fiberglassed or bolted to the inside well of the cockpit.

11. The bases of the bow pulpit are all loose and some show signs of leakage. The bases require fresh bedding compound under and tightening of the fasteners.

12. All of the cabin top handrails are quite loose and should be refastened. Not only are they leaking water into the core of the house, but they could pull loose from a person's weight and cause injury.

13. The sails have been well used and should be given to a sail-maker for the minor repairs required. Jib hanks are stiff, main-sail slides require resizing, and some chafe and broken stitching was evident.

14. The port spreader tip fitting is broken. This must be either repaired by the spar supplier by welding a new tip in place or by replacing the entier spreader.

15. The mast finish is heavily oxidized and should be cleaned.

16. The starboard upper shroud tang is badly bent and should be replaced.

17. Several of the rigging turnbuckles are frozen and require lubrication.

Conclusion

The ABC-36s, on a whole, are well built, nicely laid out cruising boats and the ILOILO is no exception. However, the majority of deficiencies herein noted can be directly attributed to both neglect and hard use. In light of this, it is my belief that the present owner owes you the courtesy of correcting these deficien-cies before such a time that you formally accept the vessel.

It is the intent and spirit of this report to provide a true and unbiased opinion of the defects of the vessel and to its equipment, elaborating on the defects and the equipment that are in need of replacement and repair. Latent defects and damages not to be found without opening up or removing ceiling, joiner work, deck coverings, fittings or tanks, etc., and/or disassembling machinery, plumbing, concealed wiring or other parts of this vessel, are not intended to be covered by this survey. The undersigned shall suffer no liability for not being able to properly evaluate parts, machinery and equipment of the hull as stated above. Acceptance of this report shall constitute agreement of the foregoing.

Respectfully submitted,

John Jones
Naval Architect
Marine Surveyor

Survey Three

April 2, 1976

Mr. A. B. Russel   File No. 1576
24 Dater Avenue
Saddle River, N.J.

Dear Mr. Russel:

This report constitutes the findings of the undersigned for a
pre-purchase survey performed on your behalf on the QXR 27,
"Kindly Light." The boat was surveyed March 31, 1976, while
hauled out and in winter storage at Mamaroneck, New York.

Year Built - 1971

Builder - QXR Yachts

Hull Registration No. - N.Y. 1234 DL

Hull No. 321

Engine Serial No. - 478571

Engine Type - Universal Atomic Four, Model UJ

General

Kindly Light is an extremely clean, well-cared-for boat that is
in very good condition throughout.

The structural integrity of the fiberglass hull and deck laminates
all appear to be quite sound. No delaminations of the hull to
deck joint, bulkheads to shell joints, or molded interior to shell
joints were discovered.

I wish to state at the time of survey, the only sail on board was
the working jib. In addition, I was unable to locate the mast,
due to its not being labeled. If arrangements can be made by
either the present owner or broker to have the remaining sails
brought to the boat and also to provide an exact location of the
mast, I will inspect them the next time I am in the area.

There were no major deficiencies found on this vessel. The following should be considered maintenance items:

1. The topsides and boot top could use a good compounding and
waxing. Doing so will clean and return luster to the gel coat.

2. The caulking seam at the forward end of the propeller strut
base requires replacement of the epoxy filler.

3. The cove stripe should be touched up in several places on the port side.

4. The toilet room sink drain sea cock is difficult to open and close. This fitting requires a good lubrication.

5. The toilet room/main cabin sliding door requires tightening of the overhead track screws, particularly on the starboard end of the track.

Conclusion

It is evident that "Kindly Light's" present owner is a meticulous person who lavished care on his boat. Although only five years old, it is still unusual in this day and age to find a boat that is in the excellent condition this vessel is. I would heartily recommend that you purchase her.

It is the intent and spirit of this report to provide a true and unbiased opinion of the defects of the vessel and to its equipment, elaborating on the defects and the equipment that are in need of replacement or repair. Latent defects and damages not to be found without opening up or removing ceiling, joiner work, deck coverings, fittings or tanks, etc., and/or disassembling machinery, plumbing, concealed wiring or other parts of this vessel, are not intended to be covered by this survey. The undersigned shall suffer no liability for not being able to properly evaluate parts, machinery and equipment of the hull as stated above. Acceptance of this report shall constitute agreement of the foregoing.

Respectfully submitted,

John Doe

John Doe
Naval Architect
Marine Surveyor

As a final note, I should say that most surveys are more like Survey Three than the other two. Boat Three is unusual mainly in her degree of cleanliness. Most used fiberglass boats have been very gently used and, therfore, are structurally sound and in need of nothing more than soap, water and wax.

9

Conclusions

Buying a boat is a little like getting married. In marrying, you don't just wed an individual, you marry an entire family. The person you marry, you might say, is just the tip of the iceberg.

Similarly, when you buy a boat you buy far more than just the boat; you buy a chain linking together individuals, things, and companies in, roughly, the following order:

The broker
The company he works for
The company that builds the boat
The boat itself

To conclude this book, I would like to make a few remarks, comments and observations under each of the above headings to indicate what you, as buyer, might reasonably look for.

The Broker

A yacht broker is a commissioned salesman. That is, he does not get paid unless and until he makes a sale. His prime interest in you at the outset, therefore, is mainly focused on the questions: Do you have the money to buy a boat? Are you likely to buy? If so, how soon?

To ferret out the answers to these basic questions, a broker probes with a number of inquiries, more or less direct. In the boat business this initial process is known as "qualifying" you as a customer — hot, warm or cool.

What I suggest you do is, while the broker is qualifying you, qualify the broker. For instance, is this man or woman a sailor, or simply a salesman? How long has he been sailing? In what? Is he a full-time broker (who will be around later to handle questions, give advice and take care of problems)? Or is selling boats just a sideline? How long has he been a broker? How long has he been a broker at the same location?

If a broker has been at the same spot for four or five years, odds are that he will continue to be there; the implication is that he is committed to this business and this company. The implication is also that he, and the company, have survived a few ups and downs, and that indicates something of the financial strength of the company and its probable ability to provide service to its buyers into the future.

Too, if the broker has been around for a while, you ought to be able to find out something about him from people you know who have bought boats in the same market area.

Now, I don't mean to make this seem like a contest or a battle. A broker has a right to be chary of his time and to prefer to spend it with people who are genuinely going to buy a boat. Most brokers are in the business because they love boats; a truly dedicated sailor who is also a broker is a mine of information which is yours once you have established a rapport.

Speaking personally and, I hope, for many of my fellow

brokers, I have learned more about boats in the eight years I have been selling them than I did in the previous twenty-two of "messing around with boats." And I am more than happy to share this knowledge with people who are genuinely interested in and sincere about buying a boat. Indeed, it's my job.

The Company

The things to look for here are touched upon in the words above: financial strength, stability, length of time in the same business at the same location. Get a Dun & Bradstreet if you can. Ask around. Take a careful look at the physical plant. Does it look like an operation that can successfully and efficiently launch and put together your new dream toy without hurting it?

The Boat Builder

Enough said, I hope, in Part 1.

The Boat

Finally, the purpose of the whole exercise: to have a boat that will serve you safely, keep you secure in all weathers and make you happy.

We are all aware of the emotional load boats carry. The two quotations at the beginning of this book give some indication of the length and breadth of the sentiment that very often is attached to sailboats. They are awfully easy to fall in love with.

This being so, the purpose of this book has not been to prevent you from falling in love but, once you've fallen, to enable you to apply rational tests to tell you whether the wench is worth it.

Basically, it is a case of knowing where to look and then comparing selected important items (such as the hull-deck joint) among the several boats that appeal to you.

It needs to be said, finally, that this whole process of finding a boat can be intensely enjoyable and educational if you use your native wit and intelligence. Sailboats are, after all, not so terribly complicated.

Indeed, that is one of their essential appeals: they realize a dream that is in many of us for a simpler, freer life. So, when you've done the work of qualifying broker, company, manufacturer and boat and found the one that best fills the bill, for heaven's sake enjoy it!

INDEX